Great Teaching

Teaching is an art that requires skill, a skill that comes by practice and as the result of long experience. But it is the skill of an artist, not of an artisan, that is required. Teaching is one of the fine arts; rather, it is the finest of arts. No other is comparable with it. All other arts deal with lifeless matter. Teaching has to do with the living soul. All other arts are perishable, this is for eternity.

Thomas J. Morgan, Principal,
Rhode Island State Normal School, from his
Studies in Pedagogy, 1888, p. 271

Great
Teaching
What Matters Most in
Helping Students Succeed

Robert C. DiGiulio

CORWIN PRESS
A Sage Publications Company
Thousand Oaks, California

For information:

Corwin Press
A Sage Publications Company
2455 Teller Road
Thousand Oaks, California 91320
www.corwinpress.com

Sage Publications Ltd.
1 Oliver's Yard
55 City Road
London EC1Y 1SP
United Kingdom

Sage Publications India Pvt. Ltd.
B-42, Panchsheel Enclave
Post Box 4109
New Delhi 110 017 India

Printed in the United States of America

Library of Congress Cataloging-in-Publication Data

DiGiulio, Robert C., 1949-
Great teaching: What matters most in helping students succeed / Robert C. DiGiulio.
    p. cm.
Includes bibliographical references and index.
ISBN 0-7619-8831-9 (cloth) — ISBN 0-7619-8832-7 (paper)
    1. Teaching. I. Title.
LB1025.3.D55 2004
371.102—dc22

2003023412

This book is printed on acid-free paper.

04   05   06   07   10   9   8   7   6   5   4   3   2

Acquisitions Editor:	Robert D. Clouse
Editorial Assistant:	Candice L. Ling
Production Editor:	Diane S. Foster
Copy Editor:	Toni Williams
Typesetter:	C&M Digitals (P) Ltd.
Proofreader:	Mary Meagher
Indexer:	Molly Hall
Cover Designer:	Michael Dubowe
Graphic Designer:	Lisa Miller

Contents

Preface

"**M**y head is spinning! There's too much to think about: paperwork, budget cutbacks, yet another new initiative, making sure the kids pass those standardized tests, getting the computers to work, trying to keep discipline in a classroom where some can't even sit still for a minute!" Three teachers were part of a discussion group I led recently, and we were talking during a coffee break (that's when the real issues surface). From that discussion, we agreed how complicated teaching seemed to be today, given all the expectations placed upon teachers and given the lack of a clear sense of what is really important to do for and with students. As I drove home from that seminar, I thought about how right they were. There seem to be two huge, but connected needs, here: First, teachers today feel swamped by tasks and expectations, so many that it is difficult to discern what is really important. They ask, "What do I do that really matters for student success?" Second, teachers have an incomplete sense of how well they are meeting those many expectations: "What am I doing well? What might I do more effectively?" At this point I felt compelled to put together a plan that would clearly address these two needs. First, teachers need to get a clearer idea of what is really important in teaching (in terms of its effects on student success). Second, teachers need affirmation about the value of what they are already doing. Addressing these two needs—for information and affirmation—formed the basis for this book.

I could attribute these teachers' needs to many causes, depending on whom I wished to blame. Principals? Do they provide leadership and support to teachers as they did years ago? Parents? Are today's parents placing too many demands upon teachers? Politicians? Do they really understand schools and education? Students? Didn't they used to come to school, sit quietly, and cheerfully await instruction from the teacher? How about my blaming video games and TV? Or the fact our society has become so complicated with a bewildering potpourri of laws, rules, policies, and special interests? We could discuss these issues and come up with some good insights. But we can also say yes, these are all true and they all contribute to the two areas of need. In the end, affixing blame is unsatisfying, for blaming does not provide teachers with help that is useful. So while the finger-pointing may continue, my book is focused on providing useful information and help for teachers and for those preparing to become teachers. It addresses two need areas: (1) helping teachers identify what good teachers do and how they do it (information), and (2) through self-assessment and collaboration, helping teachers see how what they are already doing aligns with what is essential for student success (affirmation).

For 15 years I carried out research on classrooms, teachers, and students by asking, what is it that teachers and schools do—and do not do—that matters most when it comes to our students? What helps students learn, both academically and socially? In essence, I have been asking, what is good teaching? My research has involved teachers and schools at the preschool, elementary, middle school, secondary, and postsecondary levels. It has encompassed urban and rural schools and teachers in the United States, Europe, Japan, Russia, and the West Indies. My research brought me to Finland as a Fulbright scholar examining those same questions. Originally, I began my research by observing classrooms and talking to teachers and saw some very good, great, and even heroic teachers, as well as some victims and burnout casualties. The more I probed, the more I realized it is not the age of a school, or its test scores, or the sensitivity of its metal detectors, or the number of its computer terminals, or even its funding that matters as much as the skills and qualities of the human beings who work there that make a difference. The best news is that those skills and qualities can be learned. One of my goals is to help teachers identify what those skills and qualities are and guide teachers in developing them more fully. In sum, I have tried to compose a research- and practice-based guide to the essentials of teaching from the point of view of what helps students the most.

In a sense, I am also writing this book as a historical document. I worry that the awareness of the skills and qualities that comprise great teaching is shrinking, in danger of disappearing both from the public eye and from the scope of teacher preparation. Thus, I speak not as a cheerleader of teachers but as a curator who seeks to keep alive the awareness of teachers' skills and qualities that are essential to student learning.

Teaching has existed since the first humans—generously and competently—showed other humans how to hunt, build a fire, and cook food. Good teaching has always placed the learner's needs and interests first: What was beneficial to the student—hunting, fire-making, cooking, business, or medicine—defined what was right for teachers to do. Today, what is right for teachers to do is less clear. Getting information about how to teach well is not as readily available as one may think. Once their internships and student teaching experiences have ended, teachers seldom see, hear about, or discuss models of good and great teachers in the act of teaching. Yes, there are excellent teachers out there, yet even the general public rarely hears about them. The Royal Bank of Canada issued a bank letter on the unusual subject of "The Importance of Teaching." In it, the bank wrote that "unlike sports, politics, entertainment, the arts or the law, teaching does not give rise to 'stars.' Nobody ever got a Nobel Prize for teaching achievements. . . . School teachers, as opposed to university professors, are particularly under-recognized" (1989, p. 1). The media rarely depict capable teachers whose students are succeeding—academically and socially—despite difficult conditions in their communities. Even rarer is news about real young persons who do not bring weapons to school, young persons who are not violent, and young persons who have learned how civilized human beings behave, learning much of this from skillful, caring teachers.

WHAT THIS BOOK IS AND IS NOT

I do not claim that this book is an exhaustive, all-you-ever-need-to-know-about-teaching-and-learning text. Learning—and teaching—are complex processes, and this book—any book—must of necessity be limited in its scope. However, I have tried to limit the scope to *what is most essential to teaching in terms of what helps students most*. In this book I focus not only on what are *essential behaviors and attitudes* of teaching (*essential* meaning both fundamental and valuable) but also on those essentials that are *amenable to change*. In other words, I place the highest priority on helping teachers see, think about, and improve teaching behaviors *that are largely under their control* that can be improved upon. Actually, there are many similarities between the mostly effective teacher and the mostly ineffective teacher. Both give effort to teaching, both think about students, both want to be "their best teacher"—*nobody sets out to be a bad teacher*. However, mostly effective teachers differ in that they have "a sophisticated awareness of what students do and how they think, . . . a clear command of the subject domain being taught, and . . . confidence in connecting content to the experience and background of children" (Gettinger & Stoiber, 1999, p. 937). While no single book can address "command of the subject domain" (content knowledge), it is my goal to help teachers gain that awareness and gain confidence in the best ways to connect content to students' experiences. In other words, how to teach for student success.

In addition, I am intending this book to be a useful tool for teachers' professional development, recognizing that there has been a rapid evolution in ways new and experienced teachers access professional development. Traditionally, the workshop has been the most popular format for professional development. Often led by an experienced leader or presenter who has special knowledge or expertise, workshops are typically held on teachers' inservice days, over summer or spring break, on weekends, or after school (Loucks-Horsley, Hewson, Love, & Stiles, 1998, pp. 42–43). However, recently there has been a "growing interest in 'reform' types of professional development, such as study groups or mentoring and coaching" activities (Garet, Porter, Desimone, Birman, & Suk Yoon, 2001, p. 920). Such reform activities usually take place right in school, sometimes during classroom instruction and planning time. Garet et al. (p. 921) explain that "reform types of professional development may be more likely than traditional forms to make connections with classroom teaching, and they may be easier to sustain over time . . . [and] may be more responsive to how teachers actually learn." Respected educators support the idea that reform activities may be better than other forms of professional development in terms of how successful they are in improving teaching practices (Darling-Hammond, 1995; Little, 1993). Currently, elementary, middle, and secondary schools are making greater use of reform activities in their induction programs for new teachers, as well as in professional development for their more experienced teachers. These activities include mentoring, immersion, observation of peers, in-school collaborative teams, and one-to-one coaching. It is my aim that the activities, ideas, self-assessments, and information in this book be used in the context of such reform activities and that readers use the *individual and collective wisdom and experience* of their colleagues to improve their teaching methodology.

This new way of learning sound teaching methodology means that teachers should work together, plan cooperatively, take into account the needs of their students as well as the content of the curriculum, and look at different ways teachers teach, reflecting upon reasons why they were— or were not—effective. I have designed the checklists and activities in this book to be carried out in just that reflective way because it is likely that when "teachers document and analyze their own experiences," they are engaging in the most important contemporary ways of improving teaching and learning (Wilson & Berne, 1999, p. 174). Whether one is a beginning teacher, an experienced teacher, or a student teacher, I recommend using this book collectively with other teachers and within the context of the reform model. While the checklists and activities can be profitably done by the teacher on his or her own, they are better addressed with a partner or as part of a larger, collaborative effort within the school itself.

A WORD ABOUT SCHOOLS

What do Americans want from their schools? Polls reveal that Americans say schools should teach students good behavior (socialization skills), how to get a job, and academics, in that order of priority (Galper, 1998). They say that, when today's students become adults, they should be able to succeed as well-informed citizens and contributing members of society. But how well do Americans think their schools are fostering and achieving those goals? According to the 35th Annual Phi Delta Kappa/Gallup Poll of the public's attitudes toward the public schools, 26% of Americans would give public schools in the nation a grade of A or B. However, the results are quite different when Americans rate the school they know best—their local public school. In this case, 48% grade their local school as either A or B, while 68% of parents grade the public school their oldest child attends as A or B (Rose & Gallup, 2003). Thus, those who know the local schools best give public schools their highest ratings. The poll directors conclude that "the [American] public has high regard for the public schools [and] wants needed improvements to come through those schools." The vast majority want to reform our existing schools instead of finding alternatives to those schools (Rose & Gallup, p. 42).

Nonetheless, despite this poll's positive findings, public schools still suffer from bad press, probably because people pay rapt attention to trouble ("*Does your child's school have toxic air? Find out here at NewsEleven*"). Plus there's not much one can do for a school that is working well. Gerald W. Bracey said it better: "Indeed, we must recognize that good news about public schools serves no one's reform agenda" (2003, p. 621). The tendency to castigate U.S. public education is particularly unfortunate because our schools are invaluable institutions, the best places to tackle challenges our society faces, set goals for student achievement, and teach pro-social behavior. The American Psychological Association's Commission on Violence and Youth concluded that school must play a central role, and become a leading force, in efforts to prevent antisocial behavior and violence. The commission emphasized that school-based measures be taken "to help schools provide a safe environment and effective programs to prevent violence" (1993, p. 7). As institutions, schools have several advantages in achieving these goals:

- Schools are community based; thus, they can have more of an impact than either individuals or remote government offices.
- Each school is a local school, close to and within its community.
- Schools work directly with children and adolescents.

- In terms of management, public schools are run by the public, typically an elected board.
- Schools are relatively controlled environments, and schools can provide some insulation from the world, especially valuable when that world is seen as dangerous.
- Schools are the safest of places for children and adolescents, safer than home or the neighborhood and safer than being on a bicycle or riding in an auto.
- Schools work with parents, and vice versa.
- Most of all, schools are inhabited by *people*, many of whom have the best interests of children and adolescents in mind.

Speaking of schools, the word *school* is used today as a unit of analysis, but that can be misleading. For instance, when we speak of *successful* schools and *failing* schools, we are looking at far too big a picture to make those judgments provide much meaning. In every so-called failing school are some successful students and good teachers, and in every so-called successful school are some unsuccessful students taught by not-so-good teachers. Ultimately, education reform serves students and communities best when we focus those reform efforts at the point where it really matters most: fostering good teaching for student success.

AND A WORD ABOUT TEACHERS

When I observe one of my student teachers presenting an excellent lesson, I am excited and reassured for the future. When I observe a skillful, caring teacher in action, I have hope restored.

still
A skillful, caring teacher is ^ the best resource we have to make our world a better place

American historian Henry Adams (1918) said "A teacher affects eternity." One can never tell where a teacher's influence stops. Yes, teachers are influential; we have known this since the time of the wise Buddha. But how influential is a teacher? Stanford professor Linda Darling-Hammond and research associate Peter Youngs reported "student achievement gains are much more influenced by a student's assigned teacher than other factors like class size and class composition" (Darling-Hammond & Youngs, 2002, p. 13). In arguing "how to build a better teacher," public policy researcher Robert Holland (2003) writes "teachers make a profound difference in students' lives." He advocates we focus attention on improving teacher education and view the contributions of teachers based not on their credentials but on their students' success. Supporting this idea is University of Tennessee professor William Sanders (2003), whose controversial research shows that a teacher is more important as a predictor of student success than social indicators usually identified as explanations for student failure or success:

> We've been able to get a very fair measure of the school district, the school, and the individual classroom. And we've been able to demonstrate that ethnicity, poverty, and affluence can no longer be used as justifications for the failure [of students] to make academic progress. The single biggest factor affecting academic growth of any population of youngsters is the effectiveness of the individual classroom teacher. [Furthermore], the teacher's effect on academic growth dwarfs and nearly renders trivial all these other factors that people have historically worried about.

These are strong words. Certainly, teachers by themselves cannot compensate for the damaging effects of violence, prejudice, and lack of health care upon children, especially children in poverty. Plus, educational achievement and progress are the result of a complex number of factors. But of all the factors we can more or less control, ensuring that our teachers are skillful and caring is the most significant (and cost-effective) measure we can take. Sanders points out how particularly valuable a good teacher is for minority students, who usually start out well but then tend to fall behind as they grow through elementary and middle school. He blames this fading achievement on the broad emphasis on standardized testing, which compares children to norm groups instead of comparing them to themselves. A student's academic progress should be compared to his or her previous performance and not compared to the test scores of other, quite different students thousands of miles away. Does it strike anyone as inappropriate to contrapose the test scores of Aleut children in Alaska, Latino children in Texas, Bosnian children in Vermont, and Vietnamese children in California? What educational value could possibly be derived by applying a *one-size-fits-all* mode of comparison to these diverse children? In addition, tests used in this manner cannot possibly strengthen, verify, or inform good teaching practices.

We must keep in mind that it is not tests but teachers who are key factors in student success, and this book is my effort to highlight—to bring to the foreground—those vital skills and qualities that define good teaching. I wish to do so by helping teachers recognize not only areas of needed improvement, but areas in which teachers are doing well. By focusing on *both* what they do well and what they could be doing better, teachers can become their best teacher possible. The skills and qualities I address in this book are drawn directly from what research and practice say matters most in terms of student success. It's not what looks cool but what actually *works*.

Indeed, there is a timeless aspect to the skills and qualities of great teachers. Teachers possessed these skills and qualities in ancient Greece, during the Renaissance, in South Africa during the apartheid years, and today in the United States. After hundreds of years, thousands of innovations, and incalculable technological investment, today great teaching is still great teaching. Tomorrow great teaching will still be great teaching, because great teaching is timeless. I hope this book will help keep alive those key skills and qualities and foster conversation and professional dialogue around what makes teaching *good teaching* and what makes good teaching *great*.

REVIEWER ACKNOWLEDGMENT

Corwin Press gratefully acknowledges the contributions of the following individuals:

Merle Burbridge
Consulting Teacher
Hemet Unified School District
Hemet, California

Alan S. Canestrari
Assistant Professor
Roger Williams University
Bristol, Rhode Island

Carol Mauro DiSanto
English Teacher
New York City Board of Education
Seth Low Intermediate School 96
Brooklyn, New York

Priscilla Fisk
Interim Acting Assistant Principal
Seth Low Intermediate School 96
Brooklyn, New York

Susan Gutierrez
Teacher
Forest Hills Central Middle School
Grand Rapids, Michigan

Gregg Humphrey
Elementary Teacher Education Coordinator and
Acting Director of Teacher Education
Middlebury College
Middlebury, Vermont

Susan Ohanian
Senior Fellow
Vermont Society for the Study of Education
Brandon, Vermont

Marilyn Page
Assistant Professor
Pennsylvania State University
University Park, Pennsylvania

George E. Pawlas
Professor
University of Central Florida
Orlando, Florida

Joseph Staub
Resource Specialist Teacher
Thomas Starr King Middle School
Los Angeles, California

Pam Stutzman
Teacher
Lu Sutton Elementary School
Novato, California

Gerald Tindal
Professor / Area Head
College of Education
University of Oregon
Eugene, Oregon

Diane Wolfe
Special Education Teacher Trainer
New York City Board of Education
Seth Low Intermediate School 96
Brooklyn, New York

About the Author

Robert C. DiGiulio is Education Professor at Johnson State College in Vermont. He earned his Ph.D. in human development from the University of Connecticut and recently earned his D.Ed. in socio-education from the University of South Africa. He began his teaching career in the New York City public school system, where he taught for a number of years. His 33-year career as an educator includes teaching at the elementary, middle, and college levels, with experience ranging from crowded urban schools to a one-room schoolhouse. He has also served as a school principal, educational researcher, consultant, and writer.

As an educational consultant, he codeveloped Teen Test, a vocational counseling program for adolescents. He coauthored educational computer software called Language Activities Courseware and authored its teacher's guide. His *Teacher* magazine article, "The 'Guaranteed' Behavior Improvement Plan," was recognized as having one of the highest total readership scores of any of that magazine's articles.

He has authored numerous books including *When You Are a Single Parent, Effective Parenting, Beyond Widowhood,* and *After Loss,* which was selected by *Reader's Digest* as their featured condensed book in May 1994. He is a contributing author to *The Oxford Companion to Women's Writing in the United States* and *Marriage and Family in a Changing Society* and is the coauthor of *Straight Talk About Death and Dying.*

Most recently, he has written "Nonviolent Interventions in Secondary Schools: Administrative Perspectives," a chapter in *Peacebuilding for Adolescents: Strategies for Educators and Community Leaders,* edited by Ian H. Harris and Linda R. Forcey. His most recent books are *Educate, Medicate or Litigate? What Teachers, Parents, and Administrators Must Do About Student Behavior* and *Positive Classroom Management: A Step-by-Step Guide to Successfully Running the Show Without Destroying Student Dignity,* both published by Corwin Press.

His interests include international education, child development, and teacher education. He won a 2002–2003 Fulbright Scholar Award to the University of Jyväskylä in Finland. He was a delegate to the United Nations Educational, Scientific, and Cultural Organization (UNESCO) 2003 Conference on Teaching and Learning for Intercultural Understanding. He is also a member of the Vermont Society for the Study of Education, is a life member of the Fulbright Association, and serves on Project Harmony's Advisory Board on Education Programs. He resides with his family in northern Vermont.

This book is dedicated to my grandchildren Graidy, Alex, and Sophie, and to Nona, of course.

Introduction

1

What Makes a Skillful, Caring Teacher?

Richard B. Traina, former president of Clark University, is a research historian who asked "What makes a good teacher?" (1999, p. 34). He looked through biographies and autobiographies of prominent 19th and 20th century Americans, focusing on what they had to say about qualities their best teachers possessed. Traina saw a thread that ran through their stories. First, the best teachers—the memorable ones—were remembered as being skillful and enthusiastic, having such a solid command of the subject matter that students could "pick up on their excitement" for the subject. They were knowledgeable. Second, these teachers were caring—they cared "deeply about each student and about that student's accomplishment and growth." Third, Traina said these teachers had "distinctive character. . . . [T]here was a palpable energy that suffused the competent and caring teacher, some mark-making quality." In short, memorable teachers he identified were knowledgeable, skillful, enthusiastic, caring, and special. Certainly, there is nothing unbelievable about these findings. If any of us reflect back on our best teachers' qualities, I am sure we would come up with a similar list. In 1895, Daniel Putnam (pp. 254–255), professor of psychology and pedagogy at the Michigan State Normal (teacher-training) School, said the following:

> Three things are necessary to the greatest efficiency of the work of the teacher . . . first, a thorough knowledge . . . second . . . is

a knowledge of the fundamental principles of the science of education and of the application of these principles to methods of teaching . . . [and] the third requisite . . . is genuine personality.

Over the past 100 years, many investigators have examined teacher skills and qualities that are essential to student achievement and to student socialization. For example, Charlotte Danielson has made an enormous contribution in her *Framework for Teaching*, in which she identifies and classifies aspects of teachers' responsibilities that promote student learning. She divides these responsibilities into four domains: planning and preparation, classroom environment, instruction, and professional responsibilities (Danielson, 1996). As a result of her work and the work of others, today we have a clear idea of what teaching behaviors matter most in promoting student achievement. We also know that teachers can identify and develop these skills and qualities, whether they are beginning teachers, student teachers, or experienced teachers.

GREAT TEACHING IS STILL GREAT TEACHING (AND IT'S THE TEACHING THAT MATTERS MOST!)

Sometimes teachers get bogged down. So much fills teachers' plates that it is hard to think clearly. School days are filled with reports, student needs, parental wants, administrative paperwork, curriculum meetings, standardized assessments, and many other issues. Teachers also get bogged down by distracters. For example, in looking over educational materials, books, new programs, and the like, it's easy to forget the most important factor in how well students learn is not the specific textbook a teacher uses, whether the student is placed in a single-age or multiage classroom, or how new the computer is. Educator and author Bruce Marlowe has a favorite saying whenever these types of extraneous issues and matters threaten to take on more importance than they deserve. He says, "Hey, good teaching is still good teaching." In other words, what teachers do with their students is still the most important factor in terms of student achievement. Numerous other factors, of course, also influence how well students learn. These factors include the student's innate ability, temperament, parents, home life, and socioeconomic status. Teachers and schools can't directly influence these, but having a skillful and caring teacher gives students their best shot at being successful. A teacher's skills and qualities are a variable that both teachers and school systems can address, and we should thus work toward improving the access all children have to high-quality teachers. According to Kati Haycock (1998a), director of The Education Trust, "The research could not be more clear, consistent or compelling. It supports what parents have known all along: teacher quality matters a lot. Effective teachers can help students achieve enormous gains."

Is *Highly Qualified* the Same as *High Quality?*

Haycock and others use the term *effective* as synonymous with *teacher quality*, and she frames *teacher quality* in terms of teacher effectiveness. However, this differs from what the No Child Left Behind (NCLB) Act of 2001 defines as a *highly qualified* teacher. The act defines it as a teacher who has met three requirements. The teacher (1) holds a bachelor's degree, (2) obtains full (state) certification, and (3) can "demonstrate subject matter competency in the core academic subjects the teacher teaches" (U.S. Department of Education, 2003, p. 12). This federal definition of *highly qualified* addresses a teacher's content knowledge and his or her compliance with regulations. Yes, a teacher's knowledge is important, and, yes, teachers should comply with rules for certification, yet there is a whole lot more to quality teaching than knowing a lot and being compliant! As important as knowledge and compliance are, a teacher's skills and qualities are far more significant *in terms of their effect on promoting student success and achievement.* Linda Darling-Hammond states that "measures of pedagogical knowledge, including knowledge of learning, teaching methods, and curriculum are more frequently found to influence teaching performance and often exert even stronger effects than subject-matter knowledge" (2003, p. 391). Fortunately, each state has its own requirements for teacher certification, and these requirements typically exceed the federal requirements (degree and content knowledge). Teacher skills and qualities, for example, are embedded in state-approved teacher preparation programs. These skills and qualities are also emphasized in preservice student teaching, as well as in inservice mentored teaching experiences, both of which are typical requirements for initial and permanent state certification.

In addition to its teacher-quality shortcomings, the NCLB Act is also notorious for its promotion of dire consequences for public schools characterized as *low scoring,* justifying the closing of schools as opportunities for parents to choose higher-scoring schools for their children. But identifying low-scoring ("failing") schools may be simply a pretense to reduce government spending on public education. The No Child Left Behind Act has been called "No Child Left Untested" (Ross & Mathison, 2002) due to the act's near-total reliance on identifying failing *schools* instead of failing *students* and for its broad and expensive mandate for standardized testing to legitimize that determination. As such, the act places its sights on the wrong target. Author Jonathan Kozol speaks of the damage to the teacher–student connection that is fostered by such quantitative, non-learner-centered emphases in our schools: "I'd like to see schools have no loyalty higher than their loyalty to children. I'd like to feel that the unpredictable potential of children is what we value most" (as quoted in Houston, 2000). Calling the NCLB Act little more than "empty rhetorical phrases," educators M. Donald Thomas and William L. Bainbridge (2002, p. 781) say that slogans never taught a child to read and

> neither did [sayings such as] "All children can learn." But the most preposterous of these empty rhetorical phrases is "No child left behind." The simplicity and stupidity of this statement prevent us from doing what we ought to do: Provide sufficient resources to educate all our children successfully.

This situation suggests yet another reason why focusing on becoming a better teacher is all the more urgent. Speaking pragmatically, a teacher with a reputation as a skillful and caring teacher, no matter how tight the job market may become, will always be a desired candidate, because schools are always on the lookout for the best teachers they can find. From a nobler perspective, one that will always rise above bureaucratic initiatives such as the NCLB Act, good teachers are valued because they guide students to think, and thinking people make wise decisions on matters that affect them, their families, their communities, their states, and their nation. Teachers and schools are essential to the continuance of any nation's democratic system, relying on the power of people's minds instead of the power of brute force. One of my teacher friends says she will "go through the motions with this testing frenzy" but will not lose sight of what is really important, both for her in her teaching and for her students in their learning.

"BUT WE HARDLY HAVE THE TIME!"

As I said above, teachers often have too much on their plates. But the good news is that to sharpen the skills and qualities of excellent teaching does not mean that more gets added onto that plate. Improving at teaching means that teachers should continue doing what they already do, only doing it with focus, while minimizing the time-stealers. Time-stealers are matters that wind up taking so much of a teacher's time that they do not give a good return on the investment of time and labor and do not pay off in terms of student benefit. Three quick examples are spending hours on bulletin boards, on preparing activities that are more sizzle than substance, and on troubleshooting computers. Am I saying that bulletin boards, creative activities, and computers are a waste of time? Not at all. But I am saying that these are but three of maybe hundreds of ways of spending time that do not strongly help student learning or do not help it enough to warrant the amount of time one may spend on them. Our culture today pushes a full-plate message, saying American teachers should do it all, from classroom multitasking to standardized testing and from doing a designer classroom makeover to creating all these wonderful materials, Web pages, and e-mail and telephone links with parents. Looked at separately, each is a good idea. But taken together, they can be highly stressful, they may not yield much of a return in terms of student achievement, and they move teachers further from the essence of excellent teaching. That essence is about quality, not quantity.

Axiom: Good Teaching Is Not About Quantity but Quality

Having enough time for instruction is a serious issue in today's classrooms, and the problem becomes compounded when teachers ask, Should I do *more* in order to be considered an excellent teacher? The reality is that each teacher should *not* do more, but *less*, which means shifting focus from the *quantity* to the *quality* of what is done. There's nothing worse than feeling that a lot of time was spent doing what matters not very much. Time-consuming (and time-wasting) factors cause stress. On the other hand, qualitative endeavors are less stressful (and usually make life more interesting and more fun for both teacher and student). Plus, they also make for a less-stressed classroom and better student achievement and socialization. Shifting focus from quantity to quality will not be difficult, but remember that American culture has grown accustomed to placing emphasis on the quantitative, on what can be measured, such as test scores, teachers' college degrees, number of years teaching, and other items easily tallied. These are used as quality indicators, but they are not about quality. How so? Well, for example, there is not really clear proof that the sheer amount of time students spend in classes directly results in higher academic achievement. The same is true with regard to the number of days spent in school. Increasing the total number of days students spend in school does not necessarily increase student achievement (Gijselaers & Schmidt, 1995; Walberg, 1988). Student achievement depends more on how students' time in class is used—the quality of the instructional time—than on the number of hours or days they attend (Marks, 2000). To repeat: Student achievement is a product of the *quality* of instruction far more than it is a product of the sheer *quantity* of instruction.

Given the value of instructional quality, it's particularly important for teachers to get in the habit of self-assessing. This involves reflecting on what they and their students did during the time they spent together during the school day and year. It stands to reason that as more and more stuff is placed on teachers' plates, reflection and self-assessment become more and more crucial for teachers to use to be able to move stuff *off* their plates to preserve room for what they are already doing. Otherwise, there is a danger of overload, high stress, and early burnout.

FIRST SELF-ASSESSMENT: WHAT CAN BE TOSSED AND WHAT MUST BE KEPT

There is an expression known to professional writers that helps them decide what to keep and what to do away with. Good writers know they must edit their work, and when the decisions as to what to remove become difficult, they may have to "kill their baby" and remove a phrase or section they really like, yet simply does not fit. Ouch. A harsh-sounding expression, but it applies here. Close examination and contemplation (and a good editor) help a writer realize that a section of writing must be removed entirely. It can't simply be moved elsewhere, because it just doesn't belong in the work. This removal may be painful, thus the strong expression "kill their baby." However, this process results in a stronger, more coherent work. Similarly, teachers must make an honest self-assessment and identify for removal what may be a cherished, long-standing personal practice that, upon closer examination, is not really benefiting the students or teacher. It may have once served a purpose but is now more of a time-waster, or it may be a *huge* time-waster. To make this cut calls for reflection, honesty, and courage. But the payoff will be astounding: It not only will free up more time both in preparation and in teaching but can also allow nourishment of a teacher's strong qualities and skills. As a result, students' success will be enhanced, and the teacher will be refreshed, too.

There are three opportunities for self-assessment in this book. One introductory, quick self-assessment is just ahead, with two in-depth self-assessment checklists that address key teacher skills and qualities at the end of Chapters 2 and 3, respectively. The self-assessment that lies just ahead is relatively simple and will provide insight into how to get more time out of each teaching day and how to focus on what really helps students. In other words, what can be tossed and what must be kept.

Instructions

When you have a quiet moment (or a moment to share with a mentor or colleague), take a piece of paper and list in no particular order what you did today in your role as a teacher. Brainstorm a list of at least 10 items. Do not cross out anything; there are no incorrect answers. It's important for this to be an open brainstorm, free of self-criticism and judging. Just jot down the items as they come to mind; don't elaborate, and don't explain why you did something. Allow enough time to do this, and, if needed, use another sheet of paper. (Overachievers: Stop at 100 items!)

When finished writing the list, assess it in the following way: Read each item on the list and place a plus sign (+) next to each item that involved teaching or learning and was necessary (also, mark + if it was something you were required to do, even if you did not agree with its value—for example, administering a standardized test). Place a minus sign (–) next to those items that did not directly or primarily involve teaching or learning or something you did that was not necessary to do during your school day. For example, setting up a classroom bulletin board would be a plus, since it involved teaching or learning. On the other hand, spending an hour trying to come up with an *unusually creative* bulletin board might be given a minus for being too time-consuming, as might also those personal telephone calls you made that ran longer than expected, causing you to dash to meet your students!

Here is a sample brainstormed list of a teacher's first 10 items. The list was then reviewed by its author to score each item:

LIST OF ITEMS	SCORE
Showed students how to make up note cards	+
Met with principal during morning break to discuss student	+
Volunteered for committee (said yes, but I meant to say no)	–
Took down bulletin board (students assisted)	+
Reviewed procedures and permissions for field trip	+
Made book covers for my teachers' editions	–
Set up a class debate	+
Wrote health office referral for student	+
Wrote long letter to parent (should have called, instead)	–
Listened to and assessed students' group presentations	+

Interpretation

How many items that you coded + or − gives a rough idea of the proportion of time used that directly influenced students and their learning and how much time was spent on nonessential endeavors. Hopefully, pluses outnumbered minuses.

Set up your results as follows, in a two-part format:

Give yourself a grade showing the percentage of pluses.

1. "I spent about _____% of my time in necessary or teaching- and student-related activities and about _____% of my time on matters that did not affect students' success or learning, or they were unnecessary."

My sample teacher above spent about 70% of her time in necessary or teaching- and student-related activities and about 30% of her time on matters that did not affect students' success or learning or were unnecessary.

2. "Of what I did that did not directly affect students' success or learning, or were not necessary, I could most easily dispense with the following" (list up to three items).

My sample teacher above could have declined to be on yet another committee; she could have made book covers later, at home, or not at all; and she might have telephoned the parent instead of writing a long letter.

Now come up with your percentage scores and jot down a short list of items you do that might be dispensed with. This would allow more time for instruction and learning. Repeat this self-assessment again in the near future. Having done it more than once will help make your awareness of time management more second nature. Even if you save only 20 minutes per school day, that's about 7 hours saved per month, which is *the equivalent of one full school day's worth* of extra time per month!

THE COMPLETE TEACHER: KNOWLEDGE, SKILLS, AND QUALITIES

Most teachers are skillful. They know their stuff and convey expectations for student achievement. Some expect students to rise to a high level of mastery. Others may be seen as being hard markers or even as hard people but are skillful teachers nonetheless. On the other hand, there are teachers who may be less skillful, yet they are quite caring human beings. They may show their caring in many ways, from being interested and kindhearted to wanting to be buddies with their students.

The problem is that each type of teacher in my made-up illustration is lacking what the other possesses: Some technically skillful teachers must show students their caring side, and some warm, loving teachers must sharpen their classroom teaching skills. No teacher is completely devoid of both skills and qualities, of course. If students are lucky, they will have had several skillful and caring teachers in their school experiences. They are remembered as nice people but also as complete teachers from whom students learned a lot. To be considered *complete* in most occupations, certain essentials are implied: knowledge, skills, and qualities. Whether we are talking about a hockey player, a surgeon, a chef, or a teacher, to be complete means being capable in usually more than one of these three areas. In most occupations, skills are necessary and usually so is knowledge. Hockey players, chefs, and surgeons must have both skills and knowledge. But qualities? Not necessarily. In fact, none of these three occupations requires a positive quality such as caring. Star hockey players, master chefs, and renowned surgeons can be unfriendly, obtuse, or rude; they can grow wealthy yet have an awful attitude. In the course of their employment, they are judged more on their skills and knowledge than on their caring. A teacher, however, must have all three: knowledge *and* skills *and* qualities. All teachers must possess knowledge specific to their content area. No argument there. Yet, knowledge alone—even a lot of knowledge—is never sufficient for a teacher to be considered complete. Teachers also must possess skills and qualities that help them work successfully with students. Thus, as I move ahead in this book, I will trust readers have acquired the content knowledge relevant to their teaching area, and I will focus on the other two areas: key teacher skills and key teacher qualities.

KEY TEACHER SKILLS AND QUALITIES

According to Robert Slavin, "In the past twenty years, research on teaching has made significant strides in identifying teaching behaviors associated with high student achievement" (Slavin, n.d.). These teaching behaviors include what some call "essential teaching skills," which are "basic abilities that all teachers, including those in their first year, should have to promote order and learning" (Eggen & Kauchak, 2004, p. 579). These skills are drawn from a body of educational research from the 1970s and 1980s that showed "there are specific instructional procedures which teachers can be trained to follow, and which lead to increased achievement and student engagement in their classrooms" (Rosenshine & Stevens, 1986, p. 376). Contrasted with the traditional lecture, which is a one-way monologue, there are more interactive teaching styles (Gettinger, 1995). These interactive styles foster student success, because the teacher is engaged in a continuous manner with students in an interactive fashion (Gettinger & Stoiber, 1999). The most important of these continuous-engagement behaviors of interactive teaching have a positive effect on student achievement and are what I call *key teacher skills*. These key teacher skills are *preparation, attention, clarity, questioning, monitoring, feedback, summarizing,* and *reflection.* Each key teacher skill is within the learning radar of new and experienced teachers, who can develop each to a moderate- to high-degree of proficiency. Although the key teacher skills are presented here separately, they work together in an integrated fashion with other skills. For example, a *prepared* teacher helps students focus their *attention* by asking *questions* and then provide *clear feedback* to students while *monitoring* their work. On the following pages, these skills will be described in detail, with examples provided for each skill. At the end of the next chapter are the key teacher skills checklists, developed to help teachers examine, identify, and address each personal skill area.

Although skills are important, teachers also need attitudes: frames of mind or *qualities* that predispose teachers to work well with students, which help students work well with each other and the teacher. While there are of course many qualities that can be conjured up that are relevant to teaching (such as flexibility, patience, and firmness), there are two fundamental qualities—both interrelated—that are strong predictors of student success. These are the key teacher qualities of *efficacy* and *caring.* Teacher self-efficacy (or, simply, teacher efficacy) is a teacher's belief that he or she will be effective in teaching, that is, in being successful at helping students learn. Robert Slavin calls teacher efficacy "one of the most powerful predictors of a teacher's impact on students [which] is the belief that what he or she does makes a difference" (Slavin, 2003, p. 8). Because these teachers believe their efforts will be successful, they are more resilient, persisting in the face of obstacles, and do not give up easily, trying new strategies when old ones fail.

The belief in one's efficacy is not simply wishful thinking, mind over matter, or positive self-talk. Self-efficacy is a reciprocal process of confidence: After being successful at a task, it is likely that one will approach that same task in the future with a surer sense that one will again be successful. Conversely, lack of success weakens confidence and reduces feelings of efficacy. Teachers who have been successful working with students, or even those who have simply *observed* other teachers working successfully with students, will act in ways that show they will themselves be successful. Conversely, teachers who have not been very successful, or those who have made *observations* of unsuccessful teaching, will have a weaker sense of efficacy and will act accordingly. In both cases, the beliefs that teachers hold as to the likelihood (or unlikelihood) that their teaching will be a successful endeavor will influence how teachers feel, think, and behave when actually in the act of teaching.

The second key quality is *teacher caring*, which is an interest in the student as a person, as an individual. We may see caring as affection for students, but it is more than that. Caring is concern for students that is deeper than a concern for their academic achievement, yet caring is never exploitative or directed toward the teacher's best interest. Caring respects the boundaries of intimacy, which never serve any student's (or any teacher's) best interest. Caring teachers show caring in many ways. For instance, caring teachers build and maintain a personal relationship with students individually and as a group in setting up a classroom community. Here, caring also implies the teacher taking responsibility for the classroom and then sharing that ownership with students, plus actively seeking out parents as partners, long before parents must be contacted due to a problem. In 1999, researchers Astor, Meyer, and Behre saw a striking connection between high-quality, caring behaviors by teachers and nonviolent student behavior in school. Students told researchers that teachers who showed caring did so by making "efforts to ensure students' attendance, [they] expected students to do quality work, and went beyond what the students expected in terms of personal support" (p. 24). The key teacher qualities of efficacy and caring are presented as separate entities, but the qualities work together and are woven into and expressed through teachers' skills. For example, the quality of *caring* influences the impact and value of *feedback* and *monitoring* provided by teachers to students. In a similar fashion, teachers' *efficacy* will influence how they use their *questioning* skills with students.

Chapter 2 is devoted to an examination of the eight key teacher skills and includes a key teacher skills checklist at the end of the chapter. Chapter 3 examines both key teacher qualities, with a teacher qualities checklist at the end of that chapter. Chapter 4 provides an opportunity to interpret the checklist results, with a guide to several possible self-assessment strategies.

Key Teacher Skills

What Teachers Do

Researchers and practitioners know that what teachers do—while they are actively teaching—has a positive impact on students. The key phrase is *actively teaching* because "students achieve more in classes where they spend most of their time being taught or supervised by their teachers rather than working on their own (or not working at all)" (Brophy & Good, 1986, p. 361). Other studies support the connection between teachers' skills and student achievement (Allington & Johnston, 2000; Ascher & Fruchter, 2001; Haycock, 1998b). Teacher efficacy comes into play here: A teacher's efficacy is expressed through the skills of the teacher, through what the teacher does. For example, teachers with a strong sense of efficacy will likely be well prepared and be able to use their skills in a productive way. On the other hand, lower-efficacy teachers do not anticipate they will be successful and may thus be inadequately prepared or unprepared, and this will influence their performance in the other skill areas. While there certainly are many factors that make up a successful school experience for students, what teachers do—how they use their teaching skills—will promote or diminish student achievement.

The eight key teacher skills are *preparation, attention, clarity, questioning, monitoring, feedback, summarizing,* and *reflection.* For each of these skills, teachers:

- Think about—and plan for—what they and the students will do (Preparation)
- Guide students to establish and maintain focus (Attention)

- Strive to be clear in their communication with students (Clarity)
- Ask lots of questions and invite students to ask questions (Questioning)
- Oversee student work as it is being created (Monitoring)
- Provide students with assessment that is immediate and specific (Feedback)
- Lead students to review and recap what they have learned (Summarizing)
- Contemplate instruction that has taken place (Reflection)

In the following sections, the skills will be discussed in detail, accompanied by concrete examples of each skill. Immediately following are the key teacher skills checklists so teachers can do a self-assessment of their teaching skills. After Chapter 3, which is on key teacher qualities and the key teacher qualities checklists, teachers can develop a plan to address each of the identified skills and qualities.

KEY TEACHER SKILLS, PRIOR TO TEACHING

Of the eight key teacher skills, only one—preparation—takes place before the teacher or students step into the room. As essential as each of the other seven skills are, preparation is most important, because laying the groundwork before instruction provides teacher and students with a sense of direction and purpose and increases the chances for successful instruction.

Skill #1: Preparation

A teacher's preparation to teach students is synonymous with planning: thinking about and making arrangements to follow a course of action. Early studies pointed to the value of planning, showing a relationship between teachers' planning and student achievement (see Doyle, 1977; Peterson & Clark, 1978). Later writers confirmed the connection between teacher planning and preparation and student learning (Cummings, 1990; Danielson, 1996). Of course, there is not one right way to write all plans, nor is there one type of plan for all teachers—student teachers, beginning teachers, and experienced teachers. But it is generally agreed that new, inexperienced teachers can profit from drawing up detailed instructional plans. Teachers who looked back on their early teaching experiences found that, in retrospect, such practices helped them (Clark & Peterson, 1986). For new and inexperienced teachers, detailed lesson plans provide a comfortable and useful framework to make the best use of time and serve as a guidepost for the lesson. However, even the newest and most inexperienced of teachers should never view their plans as carved in stone and should expect to gradually move away from writing detailed lesson plans. As teachers gain experience, they acquire a clearer idea of what occurs during instruction and can thus dispense with the more detailed individual lesson plans of beginning teachers.

Plans are written for instruction taking place over different lengths of time; yearly plans, for example, are written for the school year (sometimes these are *term plans* when planning for one-term blocks). Unit plans are written for blocks of time shorter than yearly or term plans, usually for a period of instruction ranging from about one week to a month. Lesson plans are written for the shortest block of time—typically for one, two, or three lessons. Here are sample formats for each of the three types of plans adapted from instructional planning formats provided undergraduate and graduate teacher education students at Johnson State College (2003–2004) in Vermont.

Sample Yearly Plan Format

Subject area, grade, or developmental level:

Students and their needs: Describe the different learning needs of students who will comprise the class. Include here the needs of, for example, special needs students, gifted students, or students who have been unsuccessful in the past. Note any special abilities, interests, or intelligences.

Goals: Typically, these are broad statements of outcomes, broader than objectives. These can be written for academic achievement and for social development.

Standards: Drawn from the state or local curriculum guide or framework of standards, these will help provide a sequence of unit topics. Learning objectives can be here as well.

Materials and resources to be used:

Assessments: What measures will be used to see growth over the year? How will you assess individual and group progress and achievement?

Typically, assessments would include formal standardized testing, but teachers should also use a variety of informal assessments such as portfolios, journals, student observations, teacher–student and student–student conference results, student self-assessments, performance tasks, and authentic assessments.

Reflection from previous years: What personal goals do you have for your teaching this year? What has worked well in the past? What could be done better this time around?

Sample Unit Plan Format

Title or topical area of unit:

Grade or developmental level, time anticipated (days, weeks?):

Objectives: What knowledge (content), skills, and attitudes should be acquired by the students? Objectives should be standards-based and connected to the curriculum. Include at least five objectives per unit plan, although for involved units more objectives would be listed.

Questions: List opening questions designed to draw in the greatest number of students, focusing questions to help students aim their attention in a direction, and probing questions that serve as continuous assessment and are presented during the teaching–learning activities.

Materials and resources needed:

Assessment: Include *initial assessment* to determine where students are at the start of the unit; *continuous assessments,* which are ongoing, where teacher and students assess and self-assess during the teaching–learning process; and *summative assessments,* tests that occur at the end of the unit to measure individual and group mastery.

Sample Lesson Plan Format

Purposes (objectives): These describe what the student(s) will do. Connections of the objectives to the state and local educational standards and curricula should be explicit.

Introduction: How will the lesson start? For example, students can be presented with a discrepant event such as an intriguing question, an apparent contradiction or paradox, or other strategy to motivate the students and help them focus their attention. What should the students know or do at the very start? Have they the prerequisite understandings or skills to be successful at this lesson?

Procedure: This is best done in a step-by-step description of how the lesson will unfold. What questions will be asked to help students focus? What degree of active involvement will be expected of students?

Formative (ongoing) check: This is a brief checking-in by the teacher as the lesson or instruction proceeds. It can be subtle, where the teacher takes a quiet moment to walk around and look at students' work, or it can be public, where the teacher asks, "Sara, what has your group learned about plate tectonics?" or "Take two minutes, turn to your partner, and take turns sharing what you've learned so far in this lesson."

Assessment: How will the teacher assess student learning in this lesson? Informal assessment is probably best if the objectives are new to the students. Questions that summarize what was done and what was learned are helpful at this point. Encourage students to ask questions and summarize thinking about "Where do we go from here?"

Reflection: This is usually done by the teacher after the lesson. Jot down what worked, what didn't work, and what will be done differently tomorrow. Reflection may also be done by students as a closing part of the lesson.

Many excellent teaching resources such as K–12 lesson plans are available free to the public online in a variety of curricular areas. For instance, standards-based lesson plans are available at the MarcoPolo Web site. MarcoPolo is a consortium of national education organizations, state education agencies, and the MarcoPolo Education Foundation. At the search page (http://www.marcopolosearch.org/mpsearch search for plans by grade level or subject area.

Planning for Student Success

Andy Baumgartner, the 1999 National (U.S.) Teacher of the Year, calls student success a "major educational issue," saying that "Every student has a right to find some element of success in his or her school career, since this is most often the major prerequisite to finding success in life." Teachers foster success by "demonstrating a high level of competency in our work" (Council of Chief State School Officers, 2003). I can add to what Mr. Baumgartner said by way of three axioms (DiGiulio, 2000, p. 49) that speak to the issue of student successes in school. These help inform teacher preparation, including yearly, unit, and lesson planning, by asking us to consider the success needs of our students:

Students who *feel* successful are seldom behavior problems.

To *feel* successful, students must actually *be* successful.

To actually *be* successful, a student must first *do* something of value.

These axioms are also helpful when we plan for students who have been unsuccessful. Students who are failing or whose behavior creates problems in the classroom (or out of the classroom) are usually uninvolved and unfocused. They are rarely successful—even though they may get praised when caught being good—because they don't actually *do something* that is of value. Some teachers simply do not get to that third axiom of ensuring students do something of value. As a result, praise their students may receive seems hollow; worse, it may be perceived as pity, weak recognition for having tried.

Before teachers can plan for students' success, they need to know a little about their students. Teachers should have a basic idea of student strengths, interests, and levels of functioning. A glance at students' past school performance can be informative, and using a simple, teacher-made diagnostic test can also help. Also, talking to and with students, individually and as a class, can provide insights into their abilities and what their likes, dislikes, strengths, and weaknesses may be.

Providing scaffolds can also help ensure student success. Scaffolding "is assistance that allows students to complete tasks they cannot complete independently" (Wood, Bruner, & Ross, 1976). Associated with Russian psychologist Lev Vygotsky, scaffolds are supports used by teachers to help learners grasp a concept or skill. Adapting materials is one type of scaffold. The gym teacher who provides a larger kickball for her younger students is making it easier for them to kick that ball. Similarly, when that gym teacher lowers the height of the basketball hoop, she is providing a scaffold by modifying the environment to help her learners be successful. Scaffolds can be verbal as well, including think-alouds, where the teacher talks through her thinking as she solves a math problem on the board in front of the class or as she walks through steps with students as they try to accomplish a complex task. Providing analogies is another type of scaffold in which students are given a parallel to what they already know in learning new information; for example, using the human brain as an analogy for a computer with its inputs, memory storage, and outputs.

Seek the point of "just-manageable difficulty." Planning for student success means gearing instruction, and student activity that accompanies that instruction, to the right level of difficulty—aiming for tasks that are neither too easy nor too difficult. Too easy is just as unhelpful as too difficult. Neither extreme aids students' feelings of success. Gettinger and Stoiber (1999, p. 942) point out "that instruction that produces moderate to high success rates (i.e., when students have a deep understanding of the material and make occasional, but few, errors) results in higher motivation for learning and better achievement." Moderate to high rates of student success increase students' self-esteem and improve students' attitudes and good behavior, and it occurs when the tasks at hand are neither too easy nor too difficult. Thus, achieving the right level of difficulty comes about when we aim for "the point of just-manageable difficulty" (DiGiulio, 2000, p. 50). This point lies just beyond our students' present level. This point s-t-r-e-t-c-h-e-s students just enough so that with personal effort and instructional support students can be successful at these tasks. Let's say there are young elementary students learning to solve simple algorithms and the teacher sees how some students are having trouble with the pen-and-paper task. She would then provide scaffolding support by using manipulatives, or she could walk them through one, speaking her thoughts aloud as she solves an algorithm. Determining where the point of just-manageable difficulty lies takes a little reflection and sensitivity to how students are grappling with the task at hand. Another way to find the point of just-manageable difficulty is to bring home students' written work, and after, skimming through it, a teacher can get a clear idea of whether it is too easy, too hard, or just right in terms of difficulty. Another way to find the point is to simply talk with students. Talk about what they do and what they have done and try to get a sense of how difficult they really felt the task was. Essentially, it's about getting to know the students as individuals.

During instruction. Preparation and planning also occur in the moment, during the act of teaching. To modify instruction as it unfolds requires flexibility. At times, teachers are afraid to deviate from plans. What results is a lesson that spirals downward, perhaps into chaos, but rarely into student success. As is the case with figuring out where the point of just-manageable difficulty lies, flexibility required for thinking on one's feet also improves with practice. Experience helps teachers trust their instincts and not continue when a lesson is not working out. At times, even the very best teachers need to stop and regroup. There is no need to draw students' attention to this shift in gears; experienced teachers shift gears with subtlety and as little fanfare as possible. For example, drawing a lesson to a fairly rapid close is one way to do this. Another way is to simply stop and take a 5-minute break with the class, moving on to something new after the break.

Flexibility means taking advantage of teachable moments. These occur when a situation spontaneously presents itself as an occasion to emphasize a point or explain some phenomenon. When I was a principal conferring with a student in her third-grade classroom, a student's seedlings, planted in a milk container, fell off the shelf and onto the floor. What did the teacher do? She reassured the child whose plant had fallen that she had planted a spare for just these moments and then proceeded to gently pick up the seedling, shaking the dirt from its roots. She called the children over to look closely at the roots, pointing out features children rarely see. (I admired her, because she made a teachable moment out of what other teachers might have called an annoying situation.) Afterward, a student swept up the mess, and that was that.

Differentiated instruction. Differentiated instruction describes ways that teachers can meet the educational needs of students with varying levels of ability and need. Preparation for differentiated instruction involves teacher reflection, as well as information and an understanding of each student. Several theories lend themselves well toward differentiated instruction. For example, Howard Gardner's multiple intelligences (MI) theory (1993) helps us see a variety of intelligences within each student. MI theory allows teachers to assess students' intelligences and plan for instruction K–12 with not the usual student needs and strengths in mind. There are many multiple intelligences assessments available online and in print. I especially value works by Thomas Armstrong, who has made MI theory very teacher usable and classroom friendly. My favorite is his book *Multiple Intelligences in the Classroom* (2000).

Teachers also differentiate instruction when they incorporate best practices for working with gifted students into the students' instructional program. For example, teachers can set up and have students use learning centers in the classroom that include challenging activities that would engage a variety of students, from regular students to gifted students. The learning centers would also help out in classroom management by arranging for students to visit these centers when, for example, they have completed their assignments ahead of others.

The individual education plan (IEP) associated with special education is another example of differentiated instruction, since it is a plan designed with the educational needs of one student in mind. For larger groups of children, differentiated instruction would include emphases on continuous assessment and use of authentic assessments, which help us go to the heart of the learning and is far superior in many cases to the multiple-choice and short-answer tests of recall. One notable work in this area is *Weaving Science Inquiry and Continuous Assessment* by Maura O'Brien Carlson, Gregg E. Humphrey, and Karen S. Reinhardt (2003). The authors do a fine job of showing how teachers can do much more than teach to the standardized test by using ongoing continuous assessment to modify their teaching and increase student success. Much of what is in the book applies to teaching outside of science as well.

Planning for positive student behavior. In planning for instruction, teachers should keep one mental eye, so to speak, on student behavior. It is no surprise to learn that students presenting challenging behaviors also tend to experience reduced classroom success (Munk & Repp, 1994). To address this means planning instruction in which student activity and involvement are built into what the students will do, allowing for little (or less than usual) amounts of hang-loose time. Knowing students and taking into account their interests will also support positive behavior and increase student success. In fact, it isn't far-fetched or irrelevant to design elementary-level lessons, early in the school year, that specifically focus on issues of behavior, classroom mutual respect, and ways of being a good school citizen, especially for students in the lower grades. In the upper grades, secondary students can profit from class discussions on such topics. Working with students with disabilities requires teachers to plan for appropriate curricular accommodations and use classroom management strategies that teach all students important academic and social skills (Allen & Burns, 1998).

For a comprehensive picture of the academic and social factors that influence student success, and a useful format to assess how a school or district meets those criteria for student success, at the end of the book under *Resources*, I have included Guidelines for Student Success in Academics and Socialization: A Schoolwide Qualitative Assessment. These guidelines can help educators (teachers, administrators, school board members, student teachers, researchers, or others) analyze key factors at the schoolwide or districtwide level that influence student academic and social success.

KEY TEACHER SKILLS, WHILE TEACHING

Six of the eight key teacher skills take place in the moment, when the teacher is in the act of instruction. Focusing student attention is the first key teacher skill.

Skill #2: Attention

In order to think and learn, people must first focus their attention (Krathwohl, Bloom, & Masia, 1964). All humans learn through their senses and thus must first attune them—pay attention—to the subject at hand. Attention is thus a valuable commodity, because it can be attuned to but one stimulus at a time: to the teacher's words, the teacher's hairdo, the clouds outside the classroom, or some deep plan for world peace. Attention is required in order to focus, and to place one's focused attention in a purposeful fashion is *to think*. Students of different ages can be taught to focus with successful learning outcomes (Beck, 1981; Harper, 1976; Lewis, Berghoff, & Pheeney, 1999), and attentional focus itself helps students see themselves as being successful learners (Wigfield, 1988).

Opening focus. In any classroom learning activity, whether teacher-led or student-led, good teachers establish student focus at the outset. Usually, teachers will do so by saying or doing something—hopefully, something interesting or meaningful to the students. Very valuable are discrepant events, which is the presentation of a dissonance or a discrepancy that comes about when something unexpected happens. For example, a science class might begin with the students observing an empty coffee can roll down an inclined plane. Ho hum. Next, the teacher releases a similar coffee can that then rolls *up* that same inclined plane! Aha! Students' attention is riveted, their mental equilibrium disrupted by this unexpected event. This is a wonderful entrée to a lesson or discussion on the properties of a cylinder or on the subject of simple machines like inclined planes. Another popular discrepant event is when a teacher dresses up like a historical character or brings in a curious prop related to the history lesson. Discrepant events bring about focus and create curiosity to learn more about the issue at hand. But even when no props are available, teachers can get students' attention by simply asking an opening question or posing a problem. (By the way, once opening focus is established, it's not a good idea to provide additional discrepant events. Once students have focused, more discrepant events can be distracting and counterproductive.)

Ongoing focus. As the lesson progresses, student focus needs to be maintained, not necessarily or even desirably focused on the teacher but on the learning at hand. Ongoing focus is needed so that students stay engaged and on task. Teachers can help students stay focused in both subtle ways (silently gesturing, pointing) and more overt, public ways. For example, ask the class that has strayed off the topic, "Where were we? Kari, can you tell us what the original problem was?" Another way to maintain focus is by the teacher simply walking around the room and visually skimming what students are doing or lending an ear to the direction of a student group's discussion. Overt, spoken reminders may be necessary, although they are not ideal since public announcements tend to throw off task students who are diligently at work. Teachers can even use a fixed-interval schedule (the good old wind-up—but now digital—oven timer) announcing that students have 8 minutes for this task, and the timer will sound when the time is up.

I attended a lecture by Howard Gardner in which he described how pleasantly surprised he was when, on a visit to China, he saw students actively and intensively engaged in high-quality ink drawings. He had wondered how such young children could produce such lovely works, but he then observed that the children were not interrupted as they worked;

no one was ringing bells; nobody came in or left for pull-out instruction. They worked, undisturbed, producing beautiful, detailed works of art. Maintaining focus is also a hallmark of Montessori classrooms, where students are given plenty of time and freedom from competing stimuli to focus on the activity at hand. Montessori students have choices, but, once a choice is made, students are expected to stay focused, supported by the Montessori environment designed especially for children (Montessori, 1966, pp. 109-110). For today's MTV generation that is used to rapidly changing colorful TV images, helping some students maintain focus can present a challenge, but even they can become absorbed by real, engaging activities within their classrooms.

High participation formats. Kounin (1970) identified high participation formats as a way of maintaining focus. This term means that lessons have a built-in high expectation of performance by students who are not directly interacting with the teacher. In other words, the lesson has something for students to do on their own *during* the lesson itself. (I emphasize the word *do*.) Instead of being expected to be passive listeners, high participation means all students have some active role to play, so they cannot sit back and let others do the work. Cooperative learning often has built-in high participation formats that help foster student success (Emmer & Gerwels, 2002). For example, Robert Slavin's Student Teams–Achievement Divisions (STAD) method of cooperative learning uses learning teams that have a mix of students "who represent a cross section of the class in past performance, race or ethnicity, and sex" (1994, p. 15). In addition, teams include a "high performer, a low performer, and two average performers," and team members work together to ensure their teammates have learned the material. High participation is built right into the very design of the STAD method. Slavin also looked at 63 studies that measured achievement in cooperative learning, and he found that in a majority of the studies, the cooperative learning groups had higher achievement than control groups. Slavin adds that, even with the use of cooperative learning activities, individual student accountability must be upheld by the teacher if the activities are to be effective (Slavin, 1994, p. 10). Another source of practical information on cooperative learning is the *Skills for School Success* series (1990–1994) by Anita Archer.

In *Inspiring Active Learning: A Handbook for Teachers* (1994), author Merrill Harmin speaks of "high-involvement lessons" that "elicit a high level of student involvement" (pp. 12–13). Harmin suggests a strategy called the Question, All Write strategy, where a question is posed to the class and students respond to the question by writing out private notes. Several students will then be asked to share their written ideas publicly, followed by a Sharing Pairs strategy, where students pick a partner and have several minutes to share with that partner what they have written or what they are thinking. The pacing of these strategies is fairly brisk, and Harmin points out that "a short discussion that zips along is better than a discussion that drags" (p. 13).

Finally, it should be noted that high participation formats are also tremendously useful in keeping students from getting into mischief. I speak from experience on this point.

Accountability. Kounin and other classroom-observing authors point to student accountability, where students know they will be held answerable for their work. Accountability helps create opening focus and maintain ongoing focus. Accountability also helps raise the quality of work students complete. If students know their work will be checked, they are more likely to complete their work. If they know their work will also be assessed or graded, students will more likely complete their work and be more accurate in their work as well. It is not necessary for teachers to collect or to grade all student work, but there should be some form of accountability for each piece of work, whether students self-check, check their partner's work, or have the teacher check their work. (This is even true with adult students in my graduate and undergraduate classes: When I announce that an assignment will be collected and checked, the quality of their work on those assignments is noticeably high.)

Skill #3: Clarity

Jere Brophy and Thomas Good (1986, p. 362) point out that "clarity of presentation is a consistent correlate of achievement," even when different types of measurement are involved. Although more research is needed into specific factors that make teaching more or less clear, the authors conclude that, "in any case, students learn more from clear presentations than from unclear ones." Clarity relates to the way teachers organize the content, how familiar the teacher is with the material, and how well "expectations and performance standards are communicated to and understood by learners" (Gettinger & Stoiber, 1999, p. 942). Other reports have described a significant relationship between teacher clarity and student achievement (Land, 1979; Rosenshine & Furst, 1973), with student satisfaction and group achievement also positively influenced by teacher clarity (Hines, Cruickshank, & Kennedy, 1982).

Clear instructions. Whether students are involved in a traditional teacher-led lesson or in a constructivist, inquiry-type activity, instructions at the outset must be stated as clearly as possible and completely stated before handing out any potentially distracting materials:

"I'm about to hand out to each student a newspaper editorial. First read it, then identify in one sentence its main point of view. Then come up with one opposing point of view."

For any type of lesson, it is essential that students listen attentively and silently while instructions are delivered. This is a practice that teachers must introduce and reinforce from day one. (I remind my student teachers they must never give verbal instructions while students are talking or otherwise inattentive. Trying to talk over student chatter will not be very effective; plus, this situation always seems to get worse when ignored by a teacher hoping that it will stop on its own. It doesn't.)

Students restate instructions. Having a student restate instructions (yes, even at the high school level) helps ensure that all students are on board. It also helps students become self-regulated learners by giving practice to developing their listening skills. Instead of the teacher repeating her own instructions, she asks a student to restate those instructions.

"Before we begin, Martina, can you please tell us what the instructions are for what we're going to do?"

"Sure. When you give us a newspaper editorial, we have to read it, then we have to think of the main idea—in one sentence—and then write an opposite viewpoint on the same subject."

Teachers can expand on a key word within the instructions as the grade and student developmental levels may warrant ("Tanya, tell us what 'controversial' means"), but it's not a good idea to go off on a tangent or start a discussion at the point where instructions are being delivered or restated.

Having students restate instructions provides feedback for the teacher on how accurately the students heard her instructions the first time, and it also gives other students reinforcement for what they are supposed to do. Plus, hearing the instructions restated allows those students who didn't get it the first time to have a face-saving second chance to get on board.

Precise terms. Clarity means using accurate words and avoiding vague words (things, guys, stuff, etc.), or what I heard a teacher say recently as she described an animal: "It was, like, omigod!" Carol Cummings (1990, p. 63) warns that *vagueness* is a threat to clarity. She cautions teachers to beware of terms such as *might, sometime, usually,* and *probably* when giving directions or instructions to students. She adds that a lack of clarity can hinder learning with "false starts, halting speech" and "uh" by the teacher. Cummings offers the following example: "Sometimes in your read . . . uh, when you pick up a book you don't know . . . I mean you encounter a diffi . . . a long word that looks like it's made up of smaller . . . er . . . a recognizable syllables. . . ." Particularly with math and science concepts that are highly abstract, use precise language to clearly convey those ideas.

Alerting. Alerting helps clarity by providing students with advance notice of transitions. For example, students are told, "In about one minute, I will call on someone to say what we know about the story so far." Alerting makes student success more likely by tipping off students of an upcoming event or transition. It allows mental preparation time.

Clear expectations. The importance of conveying clear academic and behavioral expectations to students is a practice of skillful teachers, and research shows that clear expectations are essential in creating an orderly learning environment (Cantor, Kester, & Miller, 2000; Donald, 2000). Clear expectations for school and classroom behavior, usually expressed as rules, "can reduce behavior problems that interfere with learning" (Purkey & Smith, 1983, p. 445).

The clarity with which teachers convey expectations is particularly helpful for low-ability students and minority students who are at higher risk for failure and misbehavior (Linik, 2002). These students may have difficulty understanding the classroom system and the hidden curriculum of unvoiced social expectations, especially in schools where middle-class values predominate. Minority students have difficulty discerning subtle changes in the classroom context that would signal other children to behave appropriately (Eder, 1982). Doyle (1986, p. 413) points out that "if a student's preschool or extra-school experiences do not foster understandings and behavior congruent with classroom demands, it is difficult for him or her to follow rules and procedures, gain access to instruction, or display competence."

This difficulty in following rules and expectations is minimized when teachers are as clear and explicit as possible about classroom rules and expectations for behavior (Brophy, 1996; Cartledge & Milburn, 1978; Shultz & Florio, 1979) and when teachers set up classroom procedures to be congruent with communication patterns in minority cultures. Mayer (1995) recommends that classroom rules be jointly established by the teacher and students and then integrated into the school's rules, posted in the classroom, and reviewed by teacher and students periodically.

Skill #4: Questioning

There is a link between the questions teachers ask and how effective teachers are as instructors, at all levels (Edwards & Bowman, 1996; Morine-Dershimer, 1987). All teachers ask questions; some ask quite a few: Estimates are that teachers ask between 300 and 400 questions per day

(Gall, 1970; Leven & Long, 1981)! In general, effective teachers ask lots of questions and they invite students to ask questions. In antiquity, Plato considered questioning to be the central act of a skillful teacher. Describing his teacher Socrates, Plato said that a skillful teacher is "a midwife of ideas," because just as a midwife helps the mother give birth, skillful teachers use questioning to bring forth student knowledge and under- standing (Waterfield, 1987, p. 148e–151d). Indeed, questioning serves many valuable purposes in instruction, including the organization of student thinking prior to instruction (Hamaker, 1986; Hamilton, 1985), assessment (Cotton, 1988), and determining student level of understand- ing, as well as helping the pace and momentum within lessons and assist- ing students in staying engaged (Good & Brophy, 2000; Kounin, 1970). Effective teachers also encourage students to come up with questions of their own, which helps students self-assess their own understanding and learn the instructional material at hand (Evertson, Emmer, & Brophy, 1980; Rosenshine, Meister, & Chapman, 1996). Questioning also helps teachers in their roles as constructivist educators, whereby students are not simply receivers of information but actively involved in their own learning (Wang, Haertel, & Walberg, 1993). In this constructivist context, the importance of asking the right questions *about* our students is particularly relevant for students with disabilities (Grill, 1981), where, for example, teachers need to rethink some traditional classroom assess- ment practices, such as the practice of assigning letter grades to students.

The good news about teacher skill in questioning is that, as is the case with other key teacher skills, teachers' questioning skills can be improved over time through practice and experience (Kerman, 1979; Rowe, 1986). Bloom's taxonomy (Bloom, Englehart, Furst, Hill, & Krathwohl, 1956) is an ancient but still valuable guide to questioning. It remains "the most influential scheme for categorizing questions according to their presumed cognitive level" (Cazden, 1986). Bloom's taxonomy helps teachers gauge the complexity of questions they present, as well as the complexity of classroom activities and test or quiz items. As a middle-grades teacher in New York City, to keep myself from asking too many questions at the low- est level of Bloom's taxonomy (simple recall of knowledge), I used Bloom's taxonomy. In the mail one day I received a Bloom's taxonomy "cueing bookmark" from the Language and Learning Improvement Branch, Division of Instruction at the Maryland State Department of Education (n.d.). It listed the six levels of Bloom's taxonomy, with sample questions for each level. I taped the bookmark within my visual field where I stood to teach. Using the bookmark as a sort of teaching "string around my finger" while teaching, I would quickly look at the bookmark and direct one of its "Questions for Quality Thinking" to my students. Eventually, my awareness of Bloom's levels of complexity became automatic, and I didn't need the help of the bookmark, but in the first couple of months teaching, my bookmark was invaluable. It is available online (http://www.bcps.org/offices/lis/office/inst/questthinking.html).

It looks like this:

Questions for Quality Thinking

Knowledge—Identification and recall of information.

Who, what, when, where, how? Describe _____.

Comprehension—Organization and selection of facts and ideas.

Retell _____ in your own words. What is the main idea of _____?

Application—Use of facts, rules, or principles.

How is _____ an example of _____? How is _____ related to _____?
Why is _____ significant?

Analysis—Separation of a whole into component parts.

What are the parts or features of _____? Classify _____ according to _____.
Outline/diagram/web _____. How does _____ compare/contrast with ____?

Synthesis—Combination of ideas to form a new whole.

What would you predict/infer from ____? What ideas can you add to ____?
How would you create/design a new _____? What solutions would you suggest for _____?

Evaluation—Development of opinions, judgments, or decisions.

Do you agree _____? What do you think about _____?
How would you decide about _____? What criteria would you use to assess _____?

How effective a question is, and what that question will achieve, depends on *when* in the teacher–student interaction it occurs and *what type* question it is.

When?

With respect to the timing of questioning, there are *opening questions*, *focusing questions*, and *probing questions*, each more appropriate at different times in a lesson.

Opening questions. Opening questions are meant to start a lesson or discussion and should draw in the greatest number of students. Correction: they should draw in all students. In order to draw in students and draw them in with their confidence intact, opening questions are best when they are fairly simple lower-level questions. For example, low-level opening questions can be simple recall (knowledge-level) questions such as "When we left off yesterday in our discussion of John Brown's 1859 raid at Harper's Ferry, what did we agree were the main outcomes of that raid?" or "Think about the three colors we selected yesterday for our quilt. What were those colors?" Used in this way, low-level recall questions can be surprisingly useful when teachers want to get many students on board and keep their attention (Ellis, 1993), but they are not helpful later in the lesson when teachers want to foster higher-level (analysis, synthesis, evaluation) thinking.

Focusing questions. Focusing questions are useful in guiding students where to aim their attention and can also be seen as "motivating questions" in order to "generate student interest in a lesson and to focus their attention" (Harmin, 1994, p. 89). In her effective teaching model, Madeline Hunter speaks of focus as "anticipatory set." This is where students are hooked into the objective at the start of the lesson. Hunter (1990–1991, pp. 79–80) described a sample anticipatory set and objective used in a science inquiry mode: "Let's review the procedure in making slides because today you'll be making your own slides to be used in developing a hypothesis to explain _____ and support your conclusions." This way of starting the lesson helps students focus their attention. Focusing questions can be used again at the end of the lesson to help students bring to mind what they learned from that experience.

Probing questions. Probing questions, which serve as continuous assessment, are asked during instruction to help assess student comprehension: "Kristy, tell me more about your findings. What was the most surprising result?" "P.J., what jellybeans were the least popular in our classroom?"

Probing questions can also help by *prompting* students, valuable teacher strategies that help students reply after they have given an incorrect answer or were unable to answer at all (Shuell, 1996; Brophy & Good, 1986). Examples of prompting are, "What did you notice when I tipped the upside-down glass in the water? Susan?" "I . . . I'm not sure." "What did you see?" "Air bubbles went up." However, prompting is not useful with low-level, factual recall questions such as "What is the capital of Missouri?" No amount of prompting, short of giving the student the answer, will help if the child does not know the correct answer to a knowledge-level question (Anderson & Krathwohl, 2001).

What Type?

Some types of questions invite only one right answer (convergent questions), while other questions seek a variety of possible answers (divergent questions). Convergent questions are usually lower level (knowledge and comprehension levels) and are often questions about facts: "What is the boiling point of water?" "Which treaty ended the first Napoleonic War?" "How many U.S. presidents died in office?" Convergent questions are useful by involving lower-ability students, by providing wider student participation, and by leading the way to higher-level questions. With divergent questions, think of spokes on a bicycle wheel radiating out from the center. Divergent questions ask for a variety of responses, such as opinions, predictions, and possibilities. For example, "What might happen if we used alcohol instead of water in our experiment?" "What common objects could we use to measure our height?" "Name some qualities of a good friend."

Questioning frequency. As mentioned above, more effective teachers tend to ask more questions than less effective teachers, and Brophy and Good (1986, p. 343) found that "the more successful teachers asked many more questions." Asking many questions suggests the presence of an active classroom and a classroom in which discourse is valued. Frequent questioning also implies there is momentum to the lesson or discussion. Experienced teachers don't get stuck if a line of questioning is not working out. They simply change the line of questioning instead of stopping in their tracks.

Questioning everyone. Also known as *equitable distribution,* this is when teachers direct questions to each student over the course of time and in fairly equal numbers of times. Teachers don't limit their questions to a predictable, set group of student answerers, which can serve to diminish other students' participation. When questions are equally distributed, it conveys the teacher's expectation that all will participate, that all have a chance to be part of the group, and that all can be successful. Researchers Good and Brophy (2000) add that when teachers direct their questions to a predictable, regular group of students within the class, they may be conveying expectations that are not in all students' best interests. In sum, teachers need to involve all students in the class, conveying a belief that all are expected to participate and that all are expected to learn. One way to accomplish this is for the teacher to ask a question before identifying the student who will respond. The teacher pauses after asking the question and then calls on a student or recognizes a volunteer. Since some students will never volunteer, the teacher needs to *actively* involve each student over time so that all students enjoy a role in the life of the classroom.

Wait time. After asking the class a question, it's important to wait, silently, as students think about an answer. Many teachers simply do not wait after asking a question. They wait less than 1 second for a response before turning to another student, asking a new question, or answering the question themselves. Research says that when a teacher's wait time increases—even to 3 seconds or more—students' replies will be richer and more students will participate in class (Black, 2001; Rowe, 1986; Tobin & Capie, 1980). Wait time is particularly important when teaching minority and nonnative English speaking students, because it allows them more time to process. Plus, wait time is a way of showing respect toward students. Teachers can also use wait time after a student has replied. This allows other students to piggyback—to build on an answer the first student had given. This form of wait time also increases participation and makes the discussion richer.

Inviting student questions (please!). Some recent research shows there is room for improvement in this area. Studies reveal that a lot of the classroom questioning is still done mostly by the teacher, with students relegated to asking mostly procedural and content-focused questions, with few imaginative questions asked by teachers or students (Becker, 2000). Teachers need to teach students *how to ask good questions* and then invite (require?) students to ask those questions. This would be a worthwhile activity for the first week of school: Teachers can go through the process of asking good questions, having students role-play or model some question-asking behavior. By doing this, the teacher can raise the level of discourse to share a seriousness of purpose about learning, not to the point of being humorless but to the point of a productive discussion. (At the other extreme, I have seen students ask what I call *fake questions*, questions meant to entertain others, to be silly, or to recite what they know, irrespective of the subject at hand.) By spending some time at the beginning of the school year, teachers and students can discuss what good questions are. For example, in that discussion we may agree that good questions are students' questions of curiosity, related to the topic of discussion, or students' questions that enlarge what understandings have already been set forth, building on another student's reply. In all senses, questions should be related to the subject under discussion. Questions by students are essential in all academic disciplines, but especially indispensable in science, where inquiry skills form a basis for educational discourse (Chin, Brown, & Bruce, 2002). This discourse is enriched through questioning fostered when teachers move past the "technology bandwagons" and toward information literacy (McKenzie, 2000).

Further inquiry. One lesson I learned early in my teaching career came when a principal observing my class wrote that, although I asked several good questions, in answering students' questions, he told me that some of my replies contained too much information. The principal wrote that I should "leave half-full the cup of curiosity." By that he meant teachers should not so thoroughly reply to a question that students are left over-full and overwhelmed. His point was excellent: Answer questions truthfully, but feel free to leave some of the answering to the student. It's okay to say, "Let's see if we can find out that answer." Or, "Jason, what do you think can be added to what I said?" Or, "I really don't know. Let's find out!" Respond to student questions in a way that leaves the door open for further inquiry. It helps students take charge of their own learning.

Not questioning. Teachers should be sure to spend some time *refraining from questioning* in order to help students develop their literacy skills. In his powerful book *A is for Ox: Violence, Electronic Media, and the Silencing of the Written Word*, Barry Sanders (1994) warns that many modern youngsters are missing *orality*, a "key experience" that disappears as we seek to formally educate people in reading and writing. Especially today, with our government's emphasis on standardized testing, some contemporary classrooms teach to the test, thus pushing oral language (which cannot be measured by multiple choice questions) into the background. Sanders says that orality involves the innate, natural love of the play of words that becomes abandoned as we grow through childhood and become educated:

> The teaching of literacy has to be founded on a curriculum of song, dance, play, and joking, coupled with improvisation and

recitation. Students need to hear stories, either made up by the teacher or read out loud. They need to make them up themselves or try to retell them in their own words. Teachers need to provide continual instruction in the oral arts—from primary school, through the upper grades, and on into college. Past generations were more literate because they learned to speak well and acquired an increased vocabulary through rhetorical practice. Good readers grow out of good writers and good speakers. (p. 243)

Skill #5: Monitoring

In a sense, monitoring means keeping one's finger on the pulse of the class. According to Carol Cummings, "monitoring is really a system of quality control, in which the teacher is determining whether or not each step in the teaching-learning process was effective" (1990, p. 8). A teacher's attention is trained—but moving—on the entire group of students, aware of actions, tensions, successes, failures, and social or interpersonal issues. An analogy lies in driving a car: The driver's vision and attention must be focused but should also be moving to include the road directly ahead, the left and right sides of the road directly ahead, side view mirrors, and rear view mirror (but not to the cell phone!). As a driver, these areas should be constantly monitored. Similarly, in the classroom, a teacher's eyes and attention should not stay fixed for a very long time on one person, especially during times of transition and relatively unstructured activities. Monitoring helps student success by aiding student engagement, performance, and cooperation (Emmer & Gerwels, 2002).

Looking more closely at monitoring, we see a couple of skill-related issues:

Proximity. Without getting in students' faces, teachers should avoid the other extreme of placing vast physical distances between themselves and students. Generally speaking, monitoring becomes much more difficult when teachers increase the physical distance between themselves and students. There are four distinct spatial zones in American culture (Fast, 1970). From closest to furthest, they are intimate, personal, social-consultative, and public zones, and teachers must honor their own needs and students' needs by being aware of these zones. Being in a student's intimate zone is literally getting in their face or making physical contact, which is never good for teachers to do. The personal zone (1½ to 2½ feet) can help for private teacher–student conversations or one-to-one instruction. Most teaching, however, takes place in the close phase of the social-consultative zone (4 to 7 feet). This provides a cushion, protection for students and teacher, where interaction *can* occur but is not required. Teacher and student can silently co-exist in this zone. Public distance (12 to 25 feet) is useful for formal lectures, where student–teacher interaction is minimal or nonexistent. Awareness of spatial zones is also an important consideration when teaching students from nonmainstream American cultures. Describing "how different cultures handle space," Julius Fast (1970, pp. 37–39) warns that, for example, in Japanese and Arabic cultures, "crowding together is a sign of warm and pleasant intimacy," while Westerners generally dislike closeness and desire a greater personal space. Some of these customs may have moderated since 1970, yet teachers should still use good judgment, as well as seek available resources, in order to get a sense of how closely to approach students in their classroom to reduce chances for insult or misunderstanding. This awareness is especially important in Western nations that have recently experienced an influx of immigrants from non-Western cultures.

Withitness. Kounin (1970), a keen observer of teachers, mentions with-it-ness as the degree to which teachers are aware of what is going on in the classroom. With-it-ness prevents many off-task behaviors and prevents disruption. Teachers can develop their with-it-ness by keeping their finger on the pulse of the classroom, mainly by getting close to students as they are working. Here is one way to develop a type of with-it-ness called "having eyes in the back of your head": As students work in groups, hover nearby and listen to what their group is discussing. Walk away, but without turning to look back at them, continue to listen to what that group is discussing. That's how to develop eyes in the back of your head!

Overlapping. Kounin also found that a teacher's skill in overlapping facilitated the activity flow in the classroom. Overlapping means doing two things at once: dealing with a problem or potential problem while continuing a lesson without interruption. The teacher who simply moves closer to a student who is fussing or off-task while she maintains the flow of her instructions to the class is an example of overlapping. One of the earliest examples I witnessed was in the 1950s when my aunt Flora Gigante was a school principal in the Bronx, New York. During a visit to her school, my aunt brought me into a classroom where she needed to speak to students about some upcoming event. As she spoke, I saw a boy on the side of the room spinning his pencil on the desk. Without breaking her concentration or the flow of what she was saying, my aunt slowly walked toward the boy, without breaking her eye contact on—or conversation with—the class, and simply touched his desk lightly with her finger. Shazam! To my 9-year-old eyes, it was magic; the boy stopped twirling, placed his pencil in its tray, and looked at my aunt as she spoke. This was one of hundreds of instances of overlapping that take place each day in countless classrooms. The real advantage in overlapping is that the flow of instruction and the flow of activity are not broken, with no students humiliated or otherwise getting hurt feelings.

Skill #6: Feedback

Feedback is information provided about the quality of one's work. In a recent study, the amount and type of feedback received by students influenced the quality of the content, organization, and mechanics of students' writing (Matsumura, Patthey-Chavez, Valeds, & Garnier, 2002). Teacher feedback has also been shown to improve student learning in other content areas (Blake, 1996; Kearsley, 2002; Pellett, Henschel-Pellett, & Harrison, 1994). Because feedback is information delivered to the learner—from the teacher, from other students, or from the student himself or herself—feedback is a form of *assessment*. But feedback is a type of assessment tailored to the needs of the learner, more so than standardized tests. To me, the real value of feedback lies not in what data can be reported to the state department of education or the local newspaper *but in how it can inform and help the learner, the learner's family, and the teacher* so that each may use that information toward the student's best interests. This is precisely where many believe the current standardized testing frenzy has gone awry (Brighton, 1998).

In general, feedback to students is most useful when it goes beyond students' simply knowing whether their responses are correct or incorrect (Waxman & Walberg, 1991). That information is of course important, yet the most useful feedback is specific, immediate, and contains information about what students can do to remediate, to improve their performance, or to fix a problem (and not simply hear whether it was correct or incorrect) (Butler & Winne, 1995; Kindsvatter, Wilen, & Ishler, 1988). Usually, feedback that is *positive* is, not surprisingly, very effective (Lhyle & Kulhavy, 1987; Stipek, 1993, 1996). Positive feedback can consist of simple praise ("Great job!" "Well done!"), but it's even more effective when specific: "Great job, Clarina! You remembered to include all the new vocabulary words!" or "Well done, Josh. I think Carlos feels more comfortable in our school now because of your sitting with him at lunch." Of course, negative feedback can also be helpful, provided it isn't harsh or manipulative and when it fosters self-efficacy: "Ashley, these three were incorrect, but here's a way you can check your work in the future." If feedback encourages the student to try again, to improve, it will be constructive, but if it attacks his or her feelings of being competent, negative feedback is destructive.

As a principal looking over student report cards prior to their being sent home, I pulled one card and asked the teacher to redo it. The teacher's comments to the parent were the following: "X is loud and annoying in class. He doesn't know when to be quiet, and his work is poor." I asked the teacher, Ms. Q, to try to be more positive, to write at least one little thing that X did that was positive or at least frame the negative in a way that was constructive. At first she balked, saying that "X did not deserve a good report card." Even so, I asked Ms. Q to be more informative and less harsh. Yes, she should address her concerns, but not in this way. She agreed to rewrite her comments to something like, "I am hoping X's work will improve, because he's chosen to work with a new team in class." Ms. Q also agreed to *talk* about her concerns directly with X's parent. In times like these where there is negative information to convey, the spoken word can be better than the written word.

Specific feedback. To be most useful to the student, feedback should be as specific as possible. It should relate directly to the behavior or work being evaluated (and not toward judging personal qualities of the student— saying "If only you weren't so lazy, you would be an A student" is insulting, even if in the teacher's eyes it is true). Specificity implies that feedback is detailed, where students have a clear idea of what the teacher is communicating. In a study of feedback given to fifth- and sixth-grade students, groups of students were asked to revise their compositions, but some were only told to make their paper "better," while others were told to "add at least three things that will add information to your paper" (Graham, MacArthur, & Schwartz, 1995). Not surprisingly, the students who were given the more specific feedback produced superior revisions of their original works to those given nonspecific feedback. Comments that are not specific like "Good!" or "Super!" can feel nice, but they are not as helpful as "Yes, you remembered to capitalize all the proper nouns" or "Yes, it was the 'Trail of Tears.' What was the name of the tribe?"

Immediate feedback. To be of value to students, teachers should provide feedback to students regarding the quality or value of student work *as soon as possible*—as close in time to the work being evaluated. Behavioral theory tells us that this makes feedback (reinforcement) most powerful because there is *contingency*, where the reinforcer (feedback) occurs close in time with the behavior (Kulik & Kulik, 1988). Immediacy of feedback is particularly important for younger children (Green, Fry, & Myerson, 1994), for whom later or tomorrow may as well be forever, or never.

Ongoing feedback. Feedback is effective when provided frequently: "Learners perform better and maintain high levels of academic learning time when they are given frequent feedback about their performance" (Gettinger & Stoiber, 1999, p. 941). Activities that involve learning that is very new to the student should offer ongoing feedback, while learning that is either review or connected to previous learning may have less of a need for teacher-initiated feedback, using more student-generated self-feedback as assessment. Continuous assessment, also known as formative evaluation, provides ongoing feedback for students during instruction. This maintains motivation as well as provides feedback (Olina & Sullivan, 2002). Continuous assessment also supplies valuable information for the teacher in the act of teaching. In addition to teacher-led assessments, it's a good idea to teach students how to do a continuous assessment on their own by establishing points along the way where students are given time and direction to check their progress. For example, students can be given a one-page checklist, which they keep with their supplies, and they chart their progress through an activity, a unit, or even through the day or week. This can be useful for class presentations, projects, written reports, or any number of activities.

Student self-feedback (i.e., self-regulated learning). Self-feedback is part of a larger practice called *self-regulated learning,* which is one of the more exciting initiatives in modern education. It helps answer the teacher-centered versus student-centered dichotomy that has occupied a good deal of controversy among educators by showing that, yes, the student is at the center of what teaching is all about. Self-regulated learning recognizes that as students grow, they—and not the teacher or their parents—take over primary responsibility for their learning because they have developed the skills and attitudes of a motivated learner. To be a self-regulated learner requires both *skill* and *will* on the part of the learner (McCombs & Marzano, 1990). Some students are much better than others at self-regulation, yet teachers can strive to foster self-regulation in all students, preschool through high school. Teachers can help students learn to self-regulate in the following areas: goal setting, planning, self-motivation, attention control, application of learning strategies, self-monitoring, self-evaluation, and self-reflection (Ormrod, 2004, p. 327). For example, teachers can help students judge how much time would be needed for a certain task (planning) or give the students a self-evaluation sheet upon which the student enters a comment each day regarding his or her progress (self-monitoring). Students at all levels should be shown how to self-monitor and self-assess through the use of assessments such as book conferences, portfolios, experience charts, journals, and diaries. In some of these activities, the teacher does not need to personally oversee every bit of work, particularly with journals and diaries.

Self-regulation is not really a new idea. About 100 years ago, Dr. Maria Montessori created an education method that emphasized what we today call the self-regulated learner. In *The Montessori Method* (1964, pp. 86–87), Montessori describes discipline as the learner's self-regulation, and she emphasizes the important role of the educator in fostering that quality:

> We call an individual disciplined when he is master of himself, and can, therefore, regulate his own conduct. . . . A special technique is necessary to the teacher who is to lead the child along such a path of discipline, if she is to make it possible for him to continue in this way. . . . The discipline to which the child habituates himself here is, in its character, not limited to the school environment but extends to society.

Our observations in schools in Finland showed my wife and I (and our two children who attended Finnish schools) that self-regulation among Finnish students was the most obvious quality we saw in Finnish public schools. We observed that at the beginning of the school year, American teachers have to work hard to re-create, reinvent, and reteach basic expectations for behavior and academics that Finnish educators could take for granted. From preschool through university, Finnish educators expected student self-regulation, which was supported by the Finnish social and family structure. Schools did not provide feedback through an emphasis on testing students (despite a uniform national curriculum, standardized testing is all but unknown in Finnish schools prior to the adolescent years). However, teachers in the United States are compelled to administer standardized tests (and in some districts compelled to *teach to those tests)*, even though the tests are not mainly for the benefit of students but for those far away who know little, and care even less, about *who these students are, how they learn best, and what they actually know or do not know.*

Record keeping. This is an important prerequisite skill for providing feedback. Today, parents expect that teachers keep accurate and fairly detailed records of their children's progress and achievement. Record keeping not only helps teachers formulate a grade for report cards and progress reports but also allows teachers to give students and parents (and other educators) valuable feedback on how well students are progressing. In addition to the usual teacher grade book entries, record keeping can be made alive and useful in this way: Long before teachers heard the term *portfolios*, I took a frame that held hanging files from my file drawer. I placed the frame in a cardboard box, with one hanging folder for each student, and set the box on a corner table. Beginning in September, I would now and then place samples of the students' work in the box, which was very helpful for teacher–student conferences and parent–teacher conferences. Gradually, students were also encouraged to add pieces to their folders. Best of all was when, near the end of the school year in June, I returned to students their work from the previous months. Plus, I would assign in June one or two of the same writing and math assignments they had done in September. Then I'd bring out their September work for comparison to their June work. Students were amazed to see how the quality of their work had improved over that period of time! This process also helped launch my students toward keeping records of their own work, a real step toward self-regulated learning.

Skill #7: Summarizing

Whether a teacher engages in teacher-centered or student-centered teaching, the teacher's skill in summarizing—as well as summarizing by students—can promote learning. Studies have supported the value of summarizing (King, 1992; Rinehart, Stahl, & Erickson, 1986; Thiede & Anderson, 2003), yet, from my informal observations, the greatest challenge to successful summarizing seems to be *time:* It isn't that summarizing is done poorly or unskillfully, but, mostly, it *isn't done at all!* When teachers are pressed for time, summarizing—since it typically takes place at the end of a lesson, story, or activity—may be the first thing to get dropped when the dismissal bell is 2 minutes away . . . and counting. Nevertheless, it's important to *build time into the schedule* for summarization by the teacher and by the students. Summarizing activities can grow, starting with simple discussion and recap of the lesson, afternoon, or day. For example, teachers can simply ask students to recall the important points: "In the story we just read, what do you think was the most important event? Mike?" "Which character(s) were most important?" "If we could drop a character and still have basically the same story, who could we drop?"

Once they have spent time orally summarizing from memory, students can then move on to summarizing written materials, perhaps working with a paragraph and coming up with a title or topic sentence for that paragraph. For even longer works, students can iterate the main points, perhaps numbering them and even ranking them in order of perceived importance. For example, after reading the classic children's story *Make*

Way for Ducklings by Robert McCloskey (1941), the teacher could elicit a *retelling* of the story by a student, who might reply as follows:

> A mother duck and her ducklings had to find a new home in the park in Boston for the winter. But the only way they can get there is by walking through the city. A kind police officer helps them when they try to cross the streets of Boston. They safely make their way to the park.

For older students, the summarizing or retelling would involve a more complex story and thus be in greater detail, involving character, setting, action, problem, and solution. At any age, summarization helps students separate what is irrelevant from what is important, find supporting data for main ideas, and disregard trivial or irrelevant concepts. This is not a simple task but a skill that will improve with practice. Modeling by the teacher is very valuable in teaching summarization skills. (In the *Make Way for Ducklings* example above, the teacher could summarize for the class and then read another brief story and have the students summarize that one on their own.) For all grades, teacher-guided summarization serves as a valuable model for students, since some students have difficulty summarizing; even older high school students are not necessarily proficient summarizers (Anderson & Hidi, 1988/1989).

Formative (continuous or ongoing) summary. Not all summarization takes place at the end of a lesson, on Friday afternoon, or on the last day of the unit of instruction. During the lesson, teachers should take a moment and do a formative check, asking the class, "Who can tell me what we know so far about ___?" "Where do you think the main character is headed?" (Even with young children, who may have heard or read the story countless times before, stopping and asking for a formative summary can be helpful.) Stopping and asking questions of the class can really aid student understanding, for it can confirm in students' minds that, yes, they were on the right track, and it can also help the teacher get some feedback on how well the students are comprehending: "Let's stop for just a moment. What do we know so far about the way electric currents seem to travel? Kasi?" "Anna, what did your group discover so far?" A formative check can also help students who have had a little trouble keeping up to catch up upon hearing the brief summary, realizing, "Whew, I wasn't totally lost in the woods!" A formative summary can take less than 1 or 2 minutes of class time, yet its benefits are powerful.

Chain-link summary. A good summary works both ways: It serves to close a topic, lesson, unit, or discussion, but it also works to provide a connection to what is to follow. I like the analogy of links on a chain to show that just as each link is connected on both ends, in a chain-link summary the teacher stops and asks the class to link what they are now doing with some prior but connected learning. For instance, in a lesson on *The Merchant of Venice*, the English teacher discusses its protagonist and antagonist, asking students to briefly recall these terms from an earlier play read in class, adding "How do you think *The Merchant of Venice* may differ from that play?" Through the chain-link summary, students see a link—a connection to what they already learned. They can also use a chain-link summary to predict what they might find in the conflict ahead between protagonist and antagonist, even prior to reading the play.

Set the table for next class. The time for summarizing is also a time to set the table for the following class, whether that class is tomorrow or next week. Setting the table means anticipating what the next class will use as a reference point—a connecting point to start the next class. An individual student or group of students can help promote that connection: "Shari, when we start again tomorrow, please bring up that point you made today about the Vietnam War. It's an important one that deserves more discussion."

Reviews to deepen understanding. Dempster (1991) reported that classroom reviews serve more than the purposes of repetition; they also enrich understanding, moving from surface understandings to deeper connections with the material at hand. Even a brief 2-minute, low-tech summary at the end of class or at the end of the day serves to increase the depth and extent of students' retention.

Final check-in before departure. One of the best teachers I have ever seen used this check-in as students exited his fifth-grade classroom at the end of the day. As students lined up ready to leave, Mr. A had set aside enough time right before dismissal to be able to meet each student one by one, shake hands, and check-in. As if it was a wedding reception line, Mr. A greeted and spoke with each student, and the student had to recount to him something he or she learned that day. (He said he was tired of students going home and answering "Nothin'" when asked by parents what they had learned that day.) This was his way of touching base and of also making sure there were no unresolved or simmering issues, which likely prevented a fight or two on the school bus or in the school yard. The final check-in was also a marvelous metacognitive strategy, giving each student a chance to be mindful: "Do I have everything I need?" As I saw Mr. A's class prepare to depart, I'd see a student occasionally say "Oops! Almost forgot . . ." and return to her desk to fetch a book or paper. If you see dismissal time in other classrooms as rushed and mindless, Mr. A's class was the opposite. This check-in must be planned; it can't be done as students are flying out of the room with the teacher yelling after them what the homework assignment is. I've seen that a couple of times, and that is not great summarization, to put it mildly.

KEY TEACHER SKILLS, AFTER TEACHING

Just as important as the seven previously discussed key teacher skills, what takes place after instruction completes a circle of instruction. The first key teacher skill—preparation—must be informed, of course. What the teacher does following instruction (reflection) provides the best, most accurate information for instruction that will follow. Reflection informs preparation.

Skill #8: Reflection

All teachers should contemplate their work, both after instruction and before planning. In my first year of classroom teaching, I didn't harm my students but I wasn't a very effective teacher. Looking back, it was reflection (and support from my colleague teachers) that helped me survive that first year and stay in teaching. When I got home at night, exhausted and hoarse from talking too much, I could have pushed my problems aside, watched TV, and gone to bed. This would have been understandable, but it wouldn't have helped. So I took a short nap, and, after dinner, I reflected on my day: what went well and what did not. Looking at what did not go well, I came up with new ways of addressing those challenges. One, for example, was what to do with students who were finished with their work. Upon reflection, I realized they were the ones getting into mischief. Having finished their work, they had nothing to do, so they found things to do that were not in their best interests. Some would wander and pester other students. With advice from my more-experienced peers, reflection helped me set up a system that would automatically work: Students when finished were now required to choose one of the activities I had posted near the chalkboard. No longer could students justify walking around aimlessly because they were finished and had nothing to do. I recall this success as a turning point, where I realized that yes, teaching might be the career for me. Without reflection and supportive peer teachers, I would have remained a clueless victim and probably would have quit after a year or two.

Reflection after instruction. What went well? What could work better? What needs to be improved? After instruction is a time to reflect. This can take place after the lesson (if time permits), but should take place at the end of the day. When I was principal, I asked the school board to shorten the school day (we were a half hour longer than the law required), so the teachers, staff, and I could spend that half hour together at the end of the school day, reflecting and planning collaboratively. It was a success, helping us work together and helping us be on the same wavelength in academics and behavioral expectations, and it was a time we could get to know each other and lend advice, support, and friendship. In today's huge and busy schools, the idea still applies: Teachers must reflect, both on their own and in collaboration with others.

Reflection is like a circle that includes planning for instruction, carrying out the instruction, and then reflecting and assessing the instruction and student achievement. This leads again to planning, and the cycle continues:

Planning Teaching Reflection; then the cycle repeats: Planning Teaching Reflection

How to reflect? Prove it. Experienced reflective teachers seek proof, not only from their students' work but from themselves. If something during the day went well, or it went poorly, ask for proof: What evidence is there that the math lesson bombed? Conversely, what evidence is there that it went well? Getting in the habit of proving reflections will make reflection a more powerful tool.

Long-term reflection. Reflection should also take place days, weeks, months, and even a year later. Self-questioning is the idea here: How was the past good? What was successful? What didn't work? What will I do different next month? Next year? (For reflection formats to use at different points during the school year, see "Reflective Practice for Better Teaching," Chapter 7 in *Positive Classroom Management* [DiGiulio, 2000].)

Reflective conversation. There is an excellent online resource for student teachers, new teachers, and even experienced teachers to stimulate reflective conversations. Beginning Teacher Support and Assessment (BTSA) is a California "state-funded program designed to support the professional development of beginning teachers" (Beginning Teacher Support and Assessment, 2003), and its resources are available online.

BTSA has interesting and useful information available online to facilitate a reflective conversation and help teachers grow in awareness of classroom dynamics. BTSA's plan is called Skills & Attitudes for a Reflective Conversation (www.btsa.ca.gov/ba/profdev/princ_orient/docs/ 3-02.doc). The Web page includes elements of a reflective conversation, which form the bases for building teacher efficacy and skills. These elements include good listening skills, nonjudgmental responses, and empathetic acceptance, as well as the use of questions that foster thinking and problem solving and efficacy-building measures for new teachers around issues of teacher autonomy and uniqueness. One other valuable online resource that can help teachers reflect is *Using Technology to Support Professional Reflection* by Brenda A. Dyck (2002). This resource provides directions for developing an electronic portfolio for a reflective practitioner, information on what the portfolio should contain, how to find inspiration in (online) conversations, and how to extend one's circle of influence through using online sites.

GROWING IN TEACHING: KEY TEACHER SKILLS SELF-ASSESSMENT

The following key teacher skills checklist (and the key teacher qualities checklist in Chapter 3) will help teachers complete an informal, but useful self-assessment. Teachers can use the checklists to identify and affirm what they are already doing well. Checklists can be completed at any quiet time, working alone or (even better) with a partner, mentor, or group. If it is not too threatening, teachers can profit from creating a 30-minute videotape of their teaching, using the checklists to analyze strengths and weaknesses while viewing the videotape. A trusted colleague or teacher education supervisor can help complete the self-assessment with or without the assistance of a videotape.

Remember that no teacher can ever be perfect in all eight skills. However, every teacher can (and should) rise to at least a moderate level of competency in each of the skills areas. It is likely, of course, that teachers each have relatively stronger skill areas and relatively weaker skill areas. That is one aim of the checklists: to help teachers realize what they are already doing that is good and to help teachers realize which skill areas are strong and which areas could bear improvement.

Once again, this does not require the teacher to do more than in the past. In fact, these checklists can help pinpoint what is important so that teachers can do away with what is less important and thus eliminate what may be stealing time.

Skills self-assessment, instructions. Reflecting on each indicator, try to be an objective self-observer of your teaching, not too critical nor too lenient, but straightforward and honest. As you look over the lists, think about how well or not-so-well each indicator describes what you do or how you think as a teacher. Don't dwell too long on any one indicator. Check the box in the Yes column if you now have the quality or skill described by that indicator. (Note: You may *value* a certain item, but only check Yes if you actually *do* that item.) Check Sort of if you sort of, sometimes, or moderately use that skill. In a few cases, you may need to check No if there is little or no evidence that your teaching shows that skill. If you have a trusted confidant, that person could provide a useful second opinion, helping you to see those indicators in which you excel and those indicators you need to work on.

When you have completed both the skills and the qualities checklists, look over your Yes indicators. Pick up to five indicators that most strongly (and positively) describe your teaching. Look over the Sorta and No lists. Pick one or two indicators that are items you most want to improve. Move your Yes, Sorta, and No indicators to the Summary of Skills and Qualities Checklists in Chapter 4 and proceed from there to your plan of action, described fully in Chapter 4.

Skills Checklist: Skills Indicators

	Yes	Sort of	No
Before teaching			
Preparation			
I plan for each day's schedule	☐	☐	☐
I make longer-range (unit, yearly) plans	☐	☐	☐
I plan for student activity	☐	☐	☐
I plan for student success	☐	☐	☐
I include scaffolds	☐	☐	☐
I seek the right level of difficulty	☐	☐	☐
I am flexible during instruction	☐	☐	☐
I use teachable moments	☐	☐	☐
I seek to differentiate instruction (e.g., use MI theory)	☐	☐	☐
I plan for student behavior	☐	☐	☐
During teaching			
Attention			
I create opening focus	☐	☐	☐
I maintain ongoing focus	☐	☐	☐
I work for high participation rates	☐	☐	☐
I emphasize student accountability	☐	☐	☐
Clarity			
I give clear instructions	☐	☐	☐
I ask students to restate instructions	☐	☐	☐

(Continued)

(Continued)

	Yes	Sort of	No
I use precise terms	☐	☐	☐
I use alerting	☐	☐	☐
I express my expectations clearly	☐	☐	☐
Questioning			
I ask opening questions	☐	☐	☐
I ask focusing questions	☐	☐	☐
I ask probing questions	☐	☐	☐
I use both divergent and convergent questions	☐	☐	☐
I ask questions frequently	☐	☐	☐
I question each student over time	☐	☐	☐
I allow for wait time after asking questions	☐	☐	☐
I invite students' good questions	☐	☐	☐
I enable students' further inquiry	☐	☐	☐
I do some nonquestioning	☐	☐	☐
Monitoring			
I use proximity	☐	☐	☐
I have with-it-ness	☐	☐	☐
I use overlapping	☐	☐	☐
Feedback			
I provide specific feedback	☐	☐	☐
I provide immediate feedback	☐	☐	☐
I provide ongoing feedback	☐	☐	☐
I teach students to use self-feedback	☐	☐	☐
I teach students record keeping	☐	☐	☐
Summarizing			
I provide a formative summary	☐	☐	☐
I provide a chain-link summary	☐	☐	☐
I set the table for next class	☐	☐	☐
I use reviews to aid students' understanding	☐	☐	☐
I hold a final check-in before departure	☐	☐	☐

After teaching

Reflection

I reflect immediately after instruction	☐	☐	☐
I do a long-term reflection	☐	☐	☐
I have a reflective conversation	☐	☐	☐

Key Teacher Qualities

How Teachers Are

I f knowledge is what teachers *know*, and if skills tell us what teachers *do*, then the qualities that characterize great teaching are the essential characteristics of teachers: how teachers *are*. The two key teacher qualities of efficacy and caring are qualities that directly influence student success and student achievement.

KEY TEACHER QUALITY #1—EFFICACY

In 1930, an engaging children's book was published that showed millions of children the value of self-efficacy. Called *The Little Engine That Could* (Piper, 1930), it is the story of a little train locomotive that helps a stalled train and its load of toys, through sheer determination and motivation, by pushing the heavier train up a steep incline. The action of the little train was an ideal illustration of human self-efficacy, a belief in the likely success of one's actions. Human efficacy was described by Albert Bandura (1977) in the context of social learning theory, which holds that human learning comes about through observing and then imitating models of behavior. But imitation is not mindless; people's motivation plays a role, and motivation is based upon our expectations for success at what we intend to do. These expectations are themselves based upon our prior real-life experiences, as well as upon our vicarious experiences; that is, experiences we have only witnessed in others and have not yet acted upon ourselves. (The little train engine was highly motivated, having seen other trains give a push to stalled trains. Thus it said, "I think I can; I think I can; I *know* I can!") Bandura later defined self-efficacy as "beliefs in one's capabilities to organize and execute a course of action required to produce a given attainment" (1997, p. 3).

Teacher self-efficacy (or simply, teacher efficacy) is a teacher's belief that he or she will be effective in teaching—in being a catalyst for student success. Robert Slavin adds, "Research finds that one of the most powerful predictors of a teacher's impact on students is the belief that what he or she does makes a difference. This belief, called teacher efficacy, is at the heart of what it means to be an intentional teacher" (Slavin, 2003, p. 8). Teacher efficacy "grows from real success with students, not just from the moral support or cheerleading" (Woolfolk, 2001, p. 389). Teacher efficacy is more than positive self-talk or mind over matter.

What Factors Are Connected to Teacher Efficacy?

Because the teacher–student relationship is complex, it is difficult to show a direct relationship between student achievement and teachers' personal qualities. However, there is one exception: Anita Woolfolk Hoy (Woolfolk, 2001, p. 389) found a connection between a teacher's efficacy and student achievement: "a teacher's belief that he or she can reach even difficult students to help them learn." Citing the work of Ashton and Webb (1986), Woolfolk added that a "teacher's sense of efficacy appears to be one of the few personal characteristics of teachers that is correlated with student achievement" (Woolfolk, 1993, p. 341). Others have echoed her conclusions (Allinder, 1994; Gibson & Dembo, 1984; Goddard, Hoy, & Woolfolk Hoy, 2000; Meijer & Foster, 1988; Richardson, 1990).

High- versus low-efficacy teachers. Jerome Kagan (1992) studied high-efficacy and low-efficacy teachers, finding that high-efficacy teachers accept students and the students' ideas, rely on praise rather than criticism, use their time effectively, persevere with low achievers, spend more time with them, and do not give up on them. Since low-achieving students are more likely to show antisocial and violent behavior, the teacher who sticks with a low-achieving student is benefiting the student's academic focus as well as his prosocial behavior.

High-efficacy teachers spend more classroom time than low-efficacy teachers on academic activity, and this is particularly important because the amount of classroom time students spend engaged (in academic activity) strengthens their school achievement (Doyle, 1983; Fisher et al., 1980). In the provocatively titled article "Can a Teacher Really Make the Difference?" J. R. Campbell (1974) noted a marked difference between classrooms with different activity levels. This was particularly notable in the behavior of low-ability students, where students behaved well—or poorly—depending on the level of expectation and activity by different teachers. He colorfully noted, "These problem youngsters were like a pack of hungry half-starved wolves with the math and English teachers, and like docile lambs with their science teacher" (p. 665). Campbell found that both the different expectations within different classrooms and the different activity and performance levels in those classrooms accounted for the wolves-to-lambs student responses.

In the course of my research (DiGiulio, 2001) I met several high-efficacy teachers. One was Mr. J, an inner-city teacher I interviewed. He showed very high efficacy by the way he welcomed the challenge of difficult students:

> Some teachers think that the difficult student does not want to learn. I do not believe this. I believe that all students want to learn. The problem is how to understand my students. Are you willing to change? If not, you will not be successful. I try to see the student and his behavior. As opposed to being traumatized by the student's behavior, I do not focus on the negative side. . . . [S]ome teachers spend much time analyzing negative behavior. I don't. I focus on what is positive, and encourage that.

On the other hand, some teachers do not have a strong sense of efficacy, and that also influences their performance as well as the performance of their students. Teachers low in efficacy focus more on negative sanctions (like criticism and punishments) to control students' behavior, using threats and potential penalties to motivate students. In addition, they are less likely to emphasize academics and less likely to encourage student self-regulation and self-direction. This is even true of preservice student teachers low in efficacy (Woolfolk & Hoy, 1990). In sum, "teachers who lack a secure sense of efficacy . . . tend to focus more on their own emotional distress and avoid dealing with academic problems. Thus, teachers' [sense of efficacy] affect[s] both their instructional approach and their students' level of academic success" (Gettinger & Stoiber, 1999, p. 944).

Other factors connected to teacher efficacy. In reviewing the research on teacher efficacy, Goddard and Goddard (2001) enumerated additional variables associated with individual teacher efficacy. These include:

- Organized and planful teaching
- The use of activity-based learning
- Student-centered learning

- Humanistic approaches to pupil control
- A positive association with trust
- Openness to educational consultation
- Positive attitudes toward educational reform
- Increased levels of parental involvement in schooling

Collective efficacy. But there is an even deeper meaning to the concept of teacher efficacy: An individual teacher's sense of efficacy is but a part of a larger *collective efficacy,* which is a *shared belief* (among teachers) in the likelihood of their being successful with students, who will in turn be successful (Bandura, 1977). Teacher efficacy is an individual quality, reflecting a belief that one will be successful with students, but it also is a collective quality, reflecting a belief that *we teachers* will be successful with students (Woolfolk, 1993). Individual teacher efficacy becomes even more powerful when it exists as a part of group or collective efficacy. Indeed, this sense of collective efficacy among teachers may be at the heart of the real differences between high-performing schools and low-performing schools. It is clear that levels of collective efficacy indeed do vary among schools (Bandura, 1997), and, as a result of this and other factors, schools have different student achievement outcomes. Collective teacher efficacy is not only a factor in student achievement, but it also has an even stronger effect on student achievement than socioeconomic status of the students (Bandura, 1993).

Schools that provide opportunities for teachers to interact with colleagues—to discuss matters of teaching with them—and work collaboratively with school administrators are likely to strengthen the new teachers' efficacy beliefs (Chester & Beaudin, 1996). Thus, even teachers who have only modest levels of personal teacher efficacy may be more persistent when faced with personal obstacles and setbacks *when they work in a school in which there is a high degree of collective efficacy*; that is, "where teachers tend to believe in the group's conjoint capability to educate the students successfully" (Goddard & Goddard, 2001, p. 8). On the other hand, if that same teacher were to join a faculty that has a shared sense of failure, coupled with little hope of organizational improvement, in that setting even a teacher high in (individual) efficacy may eventually come to see his or her effort, and impact, as not making much of a difference.

Teaching efficacy permeates other aspects of teaching, even outside the classroom. Teachers high in efficacy initiate contact with parents and strive to build positive relationships with the school principal and administration. Efficacy also connects with the ways teachers set up their classrooms and deliver instruction to the students. High-efficacy teachers are self-confident and self-reliant. Although they are self-reliant, they are not isolates and thus share in the school's collective efficacy. They can be said to help *make* the school a successful school. Indeed, schools can be effective institutions, and collective efficacy can be *powerful.* It can help even those students who are predisposed to violent behavior. A strong bonding to the school among delinquent and violent young adolescent boys is a significant factor in the reduction of their violent behavior (O'Donnell, Hawkins, & Abbott, 1995). The closer connection between the student and the school, the less a student is disposed to violent behavior.

What improves a teacher's efficacy? Bandura again provides some insights for teachers on this question. There are four sources of efficacy-shaping behavior: mastery experience, vicarious experience, social persuasion, and affective state (Bandura, 1986, 1997).

• *Mastery experiences.* Not surprisingly, experiences in which people perceive their performance to be at a high level of mastery lend support to their sense of efficacy. People good at golf see themselves as good golfers, and if they additionally associate with good golfers, their "good golfer" self-perceptions are strengthened. Teachers in a school where there is a collective sense of good teaching will own or share that self-perception of being a good teacher. On the other hand, a teacher in a school where teachers are generally unsuccessful will also share a low sense of mastery and have a weaker sense of efficacy.

• *Vicarious experience.* Bandura found that even when the individual does not actually act, he or she can learn through vicarious experience. Teachers who observe a model teacher at work and doing well at the task will show an increase in efficacy not only in the one doing the teaching, but also in the observer, even though the observer simply observes. The converse is true as well: Observing a teacher who is not successful lowers the efficacy beliefs of both the unsuccessful teacher and the observer (as well as the collective efficacy of the organization).

• *Social persuasion.* The teachers' room comes to mind as a meeting ground for social persuasion in schools. Teachers' rooms have been negatively (and, at times, quite accurately) characterized as dens of iniquity, where teachers sit around and complain, but teachers' rooms can also be places where teachers share encouragement and give each other valuable feedback about teaching and personal and professional support. Social persuasion affects one's efficacy for better or worse.

• *Affective state.* Affective state refers to the level of emotional arousal. For some activities, a higher level of arousal is helpful, including tasks requiring close attention, such as getting ready for a parent–teacher conference or a teacher's presentation to the school board. But in most instances where teachers work with students, arousal should be lower level in order to increase the performance of teacher and student. Constant and high levels of arousal are counterproductive and stressful to teacher and students. Both individual teachers and groups of teachers have affective states, and, depending upon what has happened to the teachers and students and what has occurred within the school, a certain level of arousal can be said to exist within both the individual teachers and the collective group of teachers. It may be a vicious circle, where groups of teachers high in efficacy can hold their sense of efficacy intact when under pressure, but those groups low in efficacy (e.g., "I'm angry because people in this town don't care about their schools!" "We have no math books as it is, and the school board is looking to cut even more.") may not, creating a vicious circle reinforcing the low sense of efficacy.

How Teachers Influence Student Success: Three Paths and One Dead End

Kind words, praise, gold stars, and the honor roll seem nice, but they do not teach students (or adults) as surely as real success experiences. Reward-maintained behavior is not well internalized, and rewards can be quite counterproductive. In his classic book *Punished by Rewards* (1993), Alfie Kohn is right on target. Using rewards can kill off curiosity and move student focus to competing instead of understanding. Kohn also points out that when students *don't* get a reward, they may actually feel punished. Successful students do not need rewards, because no reward is nearly as gratifying as when the student experiences authentic success in the classroom by doing something of value. Teachers enable this *doing something of value* in students via three paths: producing, empowering, and connecting (DiGiulio, 2001, p. 48).

Producing. We are living in a time and culture that values products, whether it is for portfolios, student placement, or teacher recognition or advancement. Student success is synonymous with the quality (and sometimes the quantity) of work students do by what they produce. This can include "participating, performing, creating, practicing, designing, producing, carrying out an experiment, finishing an assignment, or any of hundreds of other activities" (DiGiulio, 2001, p. 48). In other words, the high-efficacy teacher has students producing. Students produce best when they have assignments that are challenging but not overly difficult or simplistic. For example, asking 5-year-old children to come up with an algebraic equation is not likely to result in a producing child; similarly, asking an honors-level chemistry student to spend an hour filling in blanks on a periodic table is also not likely to result in a producing student. Misuse of worksheets can be damaging to any student's sense of having produced something of value. Usually, worksheets are mindless and require little thinking (input). The quality and value of the output, then, is quite low. Worksheets are okay for practicing and for relaxing with word-search puzzles but not for any productive and active learning.

Empowering. Student success is also fostered by teachers who empower students. We know the best leadership style for teachers is "one in which the teacher disperses as much power among the students as possible" (Shapiro, 1993). We say it, but do we do it? Dispersing power means actively teaching students how to help themselves, take responsibility for their work, get help when needed, and, in other words, how to be *self-regulating.* This means helping the student be in charge of, and responsible for, his or her own learning. But there is a caution here: It does not mean that it is beneficial when students struggle and flounder. Saying, "Sorry, but that is your responsibility" to students seeking to understand or to get on board not only leaves students cold, but it can be disempowering, especially when a student *does not know* or *lacks the knowledge or skills of self-regulation.* It is first and foremost the teacher's responsibility to teach the student *how* to be a self-regulated learner, which is a real-world skill that starts and grows in class and in school. For instance, students must learn when it is appropriate to get help from other students (in a group assignment, for example) and when it is not appropriate (during a test, for example). However, students must actively *be taught what these times are* and not simply be yelled at or punished when they seek help at the wrong time. To be self-regulated, students must also be weaned from depending on teachers to provide direction at every step. "I'm finished, Mr. D. What do I do now?" was a phrase I heard too often in my first year of teaching. I soon learned that to provide students ahead of time with choices of what to do—and the freedom and responsibility to access those choices when finished—served to empower them and free me to work with other students needing my attention.

Connecting. The third path to doing something of value lies in helping students make connections. Some people even say that's what education and learning are all about: Learning and student success are fostered by activities and assignments that connect what students already know with the activity at hand. This is the basis of *constructivism,* which is built upon the work of theorists Jean Piaget, Lev Vygotsky, Jerome

Bruner, and others. As a widely accepted model today, constructivism holds that "learners construct understanding that makes sense to them, new learning depends on current understanding, social interaction facilitates learning, [and] the most meaningful learning occurs within real-world tasks" (Eggen & Kauchak, 2004, p. 283). In other words, it is as if the learner is saying "What I learn best and fastest is that which is closest to what I already know, and I learn best what builds on what I already know. Also, I do not learn well when I try to make sense of material that is alien to what I presently know." Classrooms I observed (DiGiulio, 2001) with a constructivist orientation showed a greater degree of both student productivity and prosocial student behavior. These classrooms embraced learning more strongly than classrooms with a behaviorist (reward-and-punishment) orientation and far better than classrooms with a laissez-faire (uninvolved) teacher. Overall, the constructivist classroom facilitates the three paths to student success quite well. (For an excellent resource on constructivist teaching, see *Creating and Sustaining the Constructivist Classroom* by Bruce Marlowe and Marilyn Page [1998].)

Enthusiasm: The Great-Teacher Feature

Before I leave the subject of teacher efficacy and student success, I must add one teacher feature that lends strength to teachers' efforts in helping students succeed. That feature is enthusiasm. Teacher efficacy is strongly conveyed through a teacher's enthusiasm. When a teacher's enthusiasm is obvious to students, it helps build the students' own sense of efficacy. In fact, *teacher enthusiasm* is a positive factor from any theoretical perspective: Behaviorism says that a teacher's enthusiasm is received as positive reinforcement by the learner. Social learning theory holds that students will imitate what the teacher models—if the teacher is enthusiastic, so too will the student be enthusiastic. Cognitive learning theory says that emotions are important to the creation of new mental schemes; thus, sharing enthusiasm can be exciting and can set the stage for learning. Information processing theory says that new information will more likely find a place in the student's long-term memory when learned with pleasure, at the hands of an enthusiastic teacher. Finally, humanistic learning theory teaches that a teacher's enthusiasm can help meet students' needs for safety, belonging, and self-esteem. Indeed, teacher enthusiasm occupies an exalted throne in learning theory and in the practice of teaching. My interview with teacher Mr. J provides a clear view of a teacher's unusual thinking behind his enthusiastic approach toward working with difficult students:

The principal puts the [violent] student in my room because I appear to have the ability to deal with the most difficult students in the school. Yes, I am a male, but it is my vision for students that is different. . . . I love difficult students; my satisfaction is that if you can move a child from point A to point B, not only in mathematics and reading and science, but in behavior, then you are successful. For if you cannot change social behavior, it is more difficult to change academic behavior.

The worth of teacher enthusiasm is also supported by research. Teacher enthusiasm can help promote student achievement and mastery (Brigham, Scruggs, & Mastropieri, 1992; Carlisle & Phillips, 1984; Caruso, 1982; Perry, 1985). In their classic text *Looking in Classrooms*, Good and Brophy (2000) point out that a teacher's sincere interest and enthusiasm can help students feel that what they are learning is of value and worth their time.

The late Fred Rogers of television's *Mister Rogers' Neighborhood* was a master at conveying enthusiasm. He conveyed it in a quiet way, yet his enthusiasm (seen through his manner—his curiosity, eye contact, and smiles) was infectious. Fred Rogers showed that enthusiasm doesn't have to be loud, bubbly, or in-your-face. It can be subtle; it can be quiet. Similarly, real-life teachers can convey enthusiasm in a way that, like Mr. Rogers, arouses curiosity and a sense of wonder. Hearing someone's enthusiasm, we say, "Hmmm. Why are they so interested?" I recall a childhood friend long ago showing me his insect collection. Although I was not attracted to bugs dead or alive, I recall Gerry's enthusiasm as he pointed out insect body parts. I can still see in my mind: thorax, head, abdomen—parts I had previously only seen in books, parts I had even tried to avoid thinking about! But Gerry's enthusiasm in sharing his hobby with me caused those images and facts to stay with me today, 40-plus years afterward.

One more example of the value of teacher enthusiasm: When I was a school principal, we invited a gent to our school to teach our students mime—how to convey thoughts, feelings, and ideas without the use of words. This man was not a professional teacher but a professional clown and mime artist. In our school's lunchroom, his workshops were so engrossing that our students talked about the content long after they ended. Over time, we saw our students acting out some of the moves they had been taught outside on the playground. As I reflected on this artist with my teachers, we all agreed that his outstanding quality was his enthusiasm, which was conveyed so strongly to the students, even without the use of any spoken language. Of course, he spoke to the students at times during his workshops, but, when he spoke, he spoke of how exciting mime was to him and how he used mime to help him deal with difficulties he had as a child. He told us engaging stories of his use of mimicry in public that had all of us laughing till tears came. Mostly because of his infectious enthusiasm, this gent was indeed quite a teacher.

How Can Teachers Become Stronger in Efficacy? A Do's and Don'ts List

How can a teacher grow in efficacy and become a higher-efficacy teacher? (Perhaps the best way is to be a high-efficacy teacher to begin with and then secure a position in a high-collective-efficacy school!) But seriously, there are simple strategies and approaches both experienced and beginner teachers can use to increase their efficacy, building on and drawing from collective efficacy and helping students become successful.

Working With Other Educators

• Observe models of good teaching (other teachers). Spend time seeing how other teachers work with students. Take notes, mental or written.

• Reflect on what teachers do that fosters student success. Ask yourself, "What's going on here? Why are these students so engrossed in what they are doing?"

• Pick the brains of more-experienced teachers. Use lunchtime to unwind but also to bounce ideas off other experienced teachers.

• Ask for help or advice from other teachers. Most would be flattered if asked and more than willing to give their advice.

• Collaborate—work—with other teachers. Don't be isolated, even if the school is dysfunctional. Set up a mini-island of positive thinking teachers in a sea of negativity. Welcome others onto your island.

• Imitate—copy—what other teachers do that works. Don't get your ego involved or allow your need to be different keep you from adopting a great idea. The teacher with those great materials? That amazing lesson? She or he would probably love to share with you. Ask.

• Build positive relationships with administrators and support staff. They have a tough job, and, besides, you will never get their cooperation and help if you are angry or dismissive of them.

• Enjoy social experiences with colleagues outside of school. This can have a positive effect on the spirit within school. Have a party in your home for all the staff or all the staff in your wing or on your floor.

• Work with other teachers and staff to build a shared sense of collective efficacy. Share what the group feels is its strongpoint. Don't hesitate to take—and share and own—credit for student successes.

• Seek to moderate high stress levels through individual and group initiatives. Encourage colleagues to have health initiatives—for example, "Path to Wellness"—that build individual and group well-being.

Working With Students

Helping students be successful reinforces a teacher's sense of efficacy, and it also strengthens the students' individual and collective sense of efficacy as learners. Here are some things to do that will help both the students' and the teacher's sense of efficacy:

• Set up cooperative learning activities. Divide the day into thirds: have students spend about one-third of their time working with a partner, one-third working in a group, and one-third working solo.

• Encourage class discussions. Emphasize the importance of talking with each other by setting aside time for class discussion.

• Emphasize student responsibility. Tell students that they are accountable for their work and their behavior, and then *teach them what that means.* Don't just post rules (neat work, be safe, observe deadlines, etc.); actively model and discuss responsible behavior with the students. Also teach students *group responsibility*, including each person's obligations toward others in the class. Be sure everyone has a job to do, at least on a rotating basis.

• Teach students self-regulation (self-help and self-direction). Provide students with concrete examples of ways they are in charge of their learning (self-reporting, journal writing, self-report checklists, keeping track of their progress, portfolio building).

• Seek out parents and know them by name. Don't wait for something bad to happen as a reason to meet parents. Call, write, meet parents, and have something positive to say.

• Invite parents to participate. Even if they decline, it will show you care about them.

• Avoid sarcasm and labeling. Humor is fine, but if it's hurtful to someone, it's sarcasm.

• Convey a clear message that all students can succeed. Don't just say it; provide ways for students to be successful, even if you go outside the usual 3-Rs. Use Gardner's multiple intelligences.

• Persevere with low-achieving students. Try to help students see their progress *compared to themselves* instead of compared to everyone else in class or everyone else in America.

• Hold high but not unreasonable standards for achievement. Expect high-quality work from all students, but check in with your students and their parents to learn if it's reasonable. Too much homework? Find out.

• Choose learning activities that build on what students already know. Talk to the students to get an idea of what they know, and try to begin teaching from that point. Let them share in the instructional planning, too.

• Share personal enthusiasm for learning. Even if it's travel or a hobby, students will profit from what you describe with passion. Build in time for students to share their enthusiasm and their passions with yourself and each other.

KEY TEACHER QUALITY #2—CARING

Perhaps educators place too much emphasis on the curriculum—on the standards—and not enough emphasis on qualities such as caring. Writing in *Education Week,* teacher and literacy consultant Ardith D. Cole (2003) suggests that "successful teaching has less to do with the classroom program than with the teacher-student relationship." Skillful, caring teachers know their students as persons; they have a relationship that is professional, yet personal. In my research, I observed teachers showing caring in many ways, such as through the conversations they had with students, not only about academics but also about what was important in their students' lives. Contemporary students have different needs from students of the past. Today's students especially need teachers to be caring, given the increased number of at-risk families, the high stress of modern life, and the greater likelihood for schools to treat students impersonally. Ms. W, an urban high school teacher, told me the key element between teacher and student was "about the relationship, not the rules." She emphasized how important trust, love, and respect were, even when the student misbehaves:

> [I establish] a sense of trust, especially at the beginning of the school year. And the students must believe the teacher loves and respects them. Even if the student fails, even if a student acts disrespectfully, we have to tell him he is still loved, and there is another day.

I was fascinated by an anecdote the irrepressible Mr. J shared with me:

I was teaching conflict resolution to my class. I was teaching them how to nullify a negative statement. They were very excited about it. I told them of how I was walking by the junior high school, and this young girl looked at me and said: "You so ugly!" And I responded, "Thank you!" She said, "Why did you say 'thank you'?" I said, "Because you look at a person ugly as a negative, but I thought you looked at me so long before you concluded that I was 'ugly.'" And by using a negative statement I could become positive, and that moves them [the students].

Mr. J showed restraint, wisdom, and most of all caring in his interaction with a student who sought his attention by attempting to insult him. He turned the student's negative comment into a positive and modeled that for his classroom students.

When there is a prevailing sense among students that teachers care about them, students' needs for acceptance and being valued are met, even if those needs are not well met at home. Conversely, a lack of caring can foster overt and covert forms of violence within schools (Thayer-Bacon, 1999). Astor et al. (1999) noticed a striking connection between caring behavior by teachers and violent behavior in California high schools they examined, with no violent behavior among students when in the presence of a caring teacher. Kramer-Schlosser (1992) described the connection between high efficacy teaching and caring, and how teachers show both qualities by talking often with their students, being interested in their students' family lives and sharing information from their own lives with students. Their efficacy is rooted in their caring, in their holding of high expectations for their students, and in their use of a variety of teaching strategies to reach students. Low efficacy teachers are less interactive and at times quite authoritarian, distancing themselves from students. They see their role in helping students to succeed as being limited and place responsibility for student achievement solely on the student.

Caring teacher–student relationships also serve to "facilitate effective use of prevention and intervention methods. These trust-oriented relationships also facilitate student learning and application of alternatives to aggressive and violent behavior" (Myles & Simpson, 1998, p. 265). Myles and Simpson concluded that "educators should consistently and clearly demonstrate positive human attitudes and values toward students. In addition, educators should consistently model appropriate ways of dealing with frustration and anger." When students perceive a caring atmosphere, they respond with improved and more regular attendance, improved behavior, and higher academic achievement (Rutter, Maughan, Morimore, Outson, & Smith, 1982). Certainly, children need academic instruction to grow intellectually and to be able to secure employment in the future. However, the nonacademic socialization needs of students and society require that students experience caring relationships in school, especially those students who are at risk for antisocial and violent behavior. Unfortunately, they may not experience these caring relationships since these at-risk students (who are typically poor, Black, inner city) get less praise and positive regard than wealthier, White, middle-class, high-achieving students (Eggen & Kauchak, 2001, p. 472).

Teacher–Student Caring

Indeed, caring interventions may be particularly indispensable for the academic and social growth of U.S. student groups most at risk of failure, namely African American, Hispanic, Native American, and other minority group students. Even gang members respect teachers who expect high academic performance from them and who treat students in a caring way (Huff, 1989). When teaching culturally diverse students, "Teacher caring is also important because student perceptions of whether the teacher cares for them have a significant effect on their academic performance and behavior" (Perez , 2000, p. 103). African American students do not easily separate the person from the teacher. Perez claims that African American students are unlikely to say things like "Mr. Smith is a real bummer, isn't he? But he's a great English teacher." Thus, "culturally diverse students need a relationship with their teachers that is mutually caring and respectful if they are to learn." In order to be successful in school, students must not only like their teachers, but must believe the teacher cares about them.

The value of a teacher's personal caring relationship to students also holds true in other minority cultures. A study in rural Alaska involved almost 300 teachers, school administrators, and community members. It sought to identify qualities in effective cross-cultural teachers for Eskimo and Native American children in isolated Arctic communities. All three groups studied (teachers, administrators, and community members) identified the caring qualities of rapport, concern, and empathy most often as best evidence of teacher effectiveness (Kleinfeld, 1983, p. 1). Researchers from the University of Texas examined eight exemplary schools that served primarily Hispanic youth. These schools, located in Texas near the Mexican border, were selected because they were successful, both in student achievement and in their philosophy of education: "The schools, the parents, and community leaders jointly embraced the philosophy that all students can learn" (Ovando, 2001, p. 30). More than 90% of students were Mexican, almost 80% were poor, and most were children of migrant workers. The researchers noted the majority of teachers employed in these high-performing schools shared a Hispanic heritage with students. This may have been simply coincidental, but researchers saw a bond between teachers and children that was quite close and caring. Looking more closely at the teacher–student relationship, the researchers found "teachers treated their students as if they were their own biological children in social, emotional, physical, and academic matters. . . . [T]hey believed in contacting family members whenever it was necessary to do so." Similar outcomes were seen in a study involving exemplary teachers in England, Ireland, and the United States, where these teachers worked to get to know students as individuals, using multiple sources of information, such as dialogues and questions, knowing students informally, knowing about students from colleagues, and knowing the students' cultures (Collinson, Killeavy, & Stephenson, 1998).

Anita Woolfolk Hoy (Woolfolk, 2001, p. 463) related an anecdote about a teacher who might serve as an archetype of both key teacher qualities of efficacy and caring. She asked an educator in an urban New Jersey high school to identify which teachers work best with the most difficult students: "He said there are two kinds, teachers who can't be intimidated or fooled and expect their students to learn, and teachers who really care about the students." When Woolfolk asked "Which kind are you?" He answered "Both!"

Classrooms as a Community of Mind

The classroom must be purposely designed to bring forth positive, prosocial interactions, and this usually happens when teachers encourage in-class discussion and discourse (Schmuck & Schmuck, 1992). Jane Roland Martin, author of *The Schoolhome* (1992), believes that because society is so different today, schools must change. Martin says that schools must become more home-like and should emphasize socialization. Yes, schools should still teach the basics—the 3-Rs—but must also emphasize the 3-Cs: care, concern, and connection. Martin stresses that teachers must prepare students—male and female—for what she calls "the reproductive aspects" of society, including caring for other people, raising children, and sustaining a home. Thomas Sergiovanni (1994, pp. 127–128) recommends that schools create elementary and secondary classrooms that "resemble small family groups." He explained the key to stopping violence is to restore "a community of mind" among students. Without it, young persons substitute for this loss in violent, antisocial ways, including gang membership.

Successful teachers I interviewed or observed placed an emphasis on creating and maintaining a safe classroom community in which students and teacher respected each other. This was true irrespective of race, gender, or ethnic group of teacher or students. But unfortunately, too many American schools are not schoolhomes or small family-like groups. Indeed, some schools are prison-like. Harsh and punitive school environments can actually produce antisocial and violent behavior, bringing out aggression, as well as vandalism, and a need to escape (Azrin, Hake, Holz, & Hutchinson, 1965; Berkowitz, 1983). Western educators traditionally rely on punitive measures to maintain order and to deter misbehavior. (In about 20 U.S. states, in-school corporal punishment is legal.) However, punitive measures fail to teach anything besides fear, and they are usually applied unfairly: Punitive measures are much more likely to be applied to students who are male, students from minority groups, and students from low-income families (McFadden, Marsh, Price, & Hwang, 1992; Shaw & Braden, 1990). Teachers employed in poor areas, low-income schools, and schools where there are low percentages of White students also tend to overly rely on punishment and over use suspension and removal of students (Moore & Cooper, 1984). This finding magnifies the value of teachers who do not rely on punishment or threats but rely on their skills and qualities. I admire teachers who work under difficult circumstances, yet without resorting to punitive measures, in settings sometimes rife with aggression. Teachers I call heroic teach in the most difficult of neighborhoods, yet they describe their classrooms as places not of punishment but of shared social experiences, places that do not emphasize confrontation or competition. Significantly, their classrooms are not laissez-faire (disengaged). One teacher remarked that even the simplest of measures can help the spirit of the classroom, and the simple theme of expecting respect in the classroom was prominent among teachers interviewed. One teacher working in rural Texas told me the following:

> My classroom, to the best of my ability, I try to make it safe for everyone. I'm a firm believer that if the brain perceives threat, then you're not going to learn. By the end of the term, my classroom is a community of learners. Threats . . . aggressive behavior . . . and derogatory remarks are not allowed. It is acceptable to disagree but not acceptable to be disrespectful to anyone else.

Language of acceptance. Perhaps the best synopsis of how teachers can build a caring classroom comes from educator and writer Haim Ginott, who speaks of teachers' "language of acceptance" in his classic *Teacher and Child* (1972, p. 69). Ginott emphasizes that classroom discussion and communication have certain qualities that promote learning and prosocial behavior. His language of acceptance suggests that teachers' attitudes toward their students must not be expressed through being judgmental, hostile, or adversarial, but through acceptance. Toward this end, classroom discussions must be constructive and encourage understanding of others' points of view. Ginott points out that what the teacher does matters more than the words the teacher says. He cites examples of a classroom language of acceptance (pp. 69–99). Three relevant examples include:

• No sarcasm, no labels. While humor is an important teaching asset, sarcasm is not, nor do labels placed on students serve any constructive purpose. Sarcasm differs from humor because sarcasm hurts, bringing not smiles but pain.

• Reject the behavior, not the student. Ginott teaches teachers to separate the student's behavior from the student as a person. "Please complete your work now" addresses the behavior, while "Why don't you ever finish your work?" or "How come your homework is always missing?" attacks the person.

• Model good listening. Students will learn from teachers' behaviors more than they will learn from school rules and policies. Good listening means not interrupting students who are speaking, whether it's to the teacher, to another student, or to the entire class. It also means not allowing others to interrupt, using a gentle reminder or simply holding up an index finger that says "Hold on for one second while Amanda finishes speaking." A part of good listening is to give back what Ginott calls a "reflection" of what a student has said. For example, the teacher could paraphrase: "So you are saying that . . ." which helps both the communication and also the student, who feels like his or her words are important enough for someone to hear. In today's stressed society and classrooms, Ginott's advice on good listening is especially worthwhile.

Classroom and School Ownership: A Special Type of Caring

One inner-city teacher I met said that a solution for a school that is called "failing" is not to close it (as the prevailing federal thinking would have it), but to "Take the school back!" and have parents and community wrest control from disinterested bureaucrats or hostile student gangs. She touched on the issue of ownership, a form of caring that is relatively unresearched (Elliott, Hamburg, & Williams, 1998, p. 143), which applies not only to ownership of schools but ownership of classrooms. Today, some may object to the term *ownership*, thinking it carries an undesirably teacher-dominated nuance that may clash with a cherished ideal of a democratic classroom. But classroom ownership denotes the teacher's public sense of responsibility and accountability for his or her class or classroom (rather than exclusivity and supremacy). Astor et al. (1999) examined owned and unowned spaces in California high schools, pointing to areas in a school that are seen as unowned, such as hallways, cafeterias, and outside grounds. These are places more likely to be sites of violence. Classrooms, however, are seen as being owned (by a teacher) and are thus relatively safe places; indeed, they are the safest of places in schools. Given the value of the classroom, ownership is hence a clear form of caring by a teacher. Through a teacher's classroom ownership, students can be kept safe and empowered in the healthiest sense of the word.

In many respects, the skillful, caring teacher resembles the good parent. Since the 1960s, Diana Baumrind has studied the behavior of parents and how parental behavior affects children's development. Baumrind (1989) devised a typology of four parenting styles: authoritarian, permissive, authoritative, and uninvolved. Authoritative parents set limits but also emphasize fairness and mutuality, providing a positive model for their child. Just as authoritative parents were most effective in Baumrind's typology, authoritative teachers are also most effective. Inner-city high school teacher Mr. K was one example. Like Mr. J, Mr. K was so effective, particularly with misbehaving students, that his school's principal as a matter of course placed children who had been expelled from other classrooms in Mr. K's room. Since Mr. K had clear classroom ownership, the introduction of a potentially violent student into his classroom did not jeopardize the other students. Mr. K handled students with love, but very firmly. He joked with me at the end of his interview: "I don't know if I am a very good candidate to discuss school violence, because I tend to nip it in the bud."

Similar to Mr. K and Mr. J was Ms. R, a suburban high school teacher who made it clear to me, and to all listeners, that she owned her classroom:

> Children will test teachers. Reputation is very important. There are some teachers who have a reputation of letting anything go. There are some teachers who set the ground rules. I set the ground rules on day one. I tell the students: "I have only one rule for you to remember. And that rule is 'I Win.'" . . . [smiling] I have a reputation of being tough but fair.

Certainly, teachers have a powerful effect on student achievement and behavior when they create a safe environment. Especially in schools and classrooms with racially and ethnically diverse children, we cannot simply throw students together in a classroom and have that diversity by itself yield a positive effect (Schmuck & Schmuck, 1992). The creation and maintenance of a positive classroom context must be a deliberate act on the teacher's part. The teacher must *purposefully build* a warm and constructive classroom context (Shechtman, 1997).

Caring Means Parents, Too: Parental Involvement and Support

An abundance of research (and common sense) says that parents' interest in their child's education plays a key role in the child's learning and has a beneficial effect upon the child's behavior. Researchers Myles and Simpson (1998, p. 266) found that "Parents and families play an important role in supporting children and youth with problems of aggression and violence. In fact, parent and family support systems are often the bridge to long-term solutions to problems of aggression and violence." In addition to their effect upon violent behavior, these support systems influence the self-concept of children and adolescents. Parental support for learning increases the positive self-concepts of adolescents: When parents are interested in their child's education, the child's self-concept is strengthened (Marjoribanks & Mboya, 1998). Teachers play a crucial role in fostering this parental support for learning by proactively reaching out to parents. After a comprehensive review of factors affecting student achievement and learning, Wang et al. (1993, pp. 278–279) concluded that "teachers must also develop strategies to increase parent involvement in their children's academic life. This means teachers should go beyond traditional once-a-year parent/teacher conferences and work with parents to see that learning is valued in the home." I found that high-efficacy teachers not only acknowledged the importance of parental involvement, but *they also reached out for parents* through conferences, telephone calls, and even mailing letters to maintain communication with parents and to let parents know how well their children were progressing in school. Of all technology available to today's teacher, the best is still the telephone, which can provide an immediate connection (unlike e-mail and handwritten letters). The telephone can be a particularly useful tool if home visits may be unsafe or too distant, valuable when parents and teachers have busy schedules. A telephone call to parents—simply to introduce one's self—strongly communicates caring, and it also allows teachers to be more clearly understood in describing a student's needs.

All children are at risk for stress when they live in a home headed by a single parent. Minority group children (including African American children) are at an increased risk for academic and social failure when they live in a single-parent home (Luster & McAdoo, 1994). These children tend to perform more poorly in school, and they are more predisposed toward problem behaviors when compared to their peers living in two-parent homes. This makes parental support provided by teachers especially beneficial for this vulnerable group of children. Closeness with parents also benefits the teacher's efficacy: Teachers who seek to involve parents are also more positive toward teaching and are more favorably inclined toward their school than teachers who do not seek out parents (Epstein, 1990).

How Can Teachers Become Stronger in Caring? A Do's and Don'ts List

The following list is a summary of caring teacher behaviors that influence student success, both academic success and social success. The behaviors form the bases for the checklist to follow.

• Avoid harsh, punitive measures. Yes, fear works, because people *comply* when they are fearful, but they do not *learn* best in that condition.

• Reject behavior, not the student. Instead of saying "Why do you always do that?" speak about the behavior instead of the accusatory "you."

• Nip misbehavior in the bud. Try not to get in the habit of ignoring misbehavior. It will continue and grow unless dealt with promptly.

• Model reflective listening. This means not thinking of something else when students talk with you and giving them your full attention.

• Look at students when they speak. Give them your eyes as well as your ears to let them *see* you are listening.

• Expect students to respect you, each other, and themselves. Act as if it is the most normal thing in the world and nothing unusual that students respect you, you respect your students, and you expect them to respect each other.

• Know students as individuals; know them by name. When handing papers back, say the students' names as they reach for their paper.

- Emphasize relationships over rules. A teacher acting like a judge and jury in the classroom isn't helpful unless teachers have a lock-up where the guilty party can be sent. Talk positively; talk about how students can get along instead of seeking to affix blame.

- Talk often with students inside and outside of class. Talk informally with students about real things.

- Be interested in students' lives outside of school. Take an interest in what they do outside school because that may be where they feel really successful (or not).

- Try to use a variety of teaching strategies. Keep students on their toes by being unpredictable with a combination of hands-on, discussion, lecture (a little), guests, and field research instead of the same old thing each day.

- Model for students appropriate ways to deal with frustration. They are looking at you, always.

- Teach students how to resolve differences. Teach that conflict is a chance to problem solve, instead of an I-win/you-lose contest.

- Model respect in the classroom. Act respectfully toward students.

- Model courteous speech. Use humor, but avoid harshness and vulgarity, even if students hear worse language on TV. Teachers are real, TV is not. Besides, teachers must be better than TV.

- Model concern and empathy. It's okay to have feelings but share them without making your feelings the center of the student's day.

GROWING IN TEACHING: KEY TEACHER QUALITIES SELF-ASSESSMENT

The following qualities checklists will help you complete an informal but useful self-assessment. As you did with the skills checklist, use the qualities checklists to help affirm what you are already doing well. If you have already completed the skills checklist, proceed to the next section and complete the qualities checklists. If not, see the instructions for completing the skills checklist at the end of Chapter 2. The procedure is the same for the qualities checklists that follow.

Qualities Checklist: Efficacy Indicators

	Yes	Sort of	No
Working with colleagues, I			
Observe models of good teaching (other teachers)	☐	☐	☐
Reflect on what teachers do that fosters student success	☐	☐	☐
Pick the brains of more experienced teachers	☐	☐	☐
Ask for help or advice from other teachers	☐	☐	☐
Collaborate—work—with other teachers	☐	☐	☐
Imitate—copy—what other teachers do that works	☐	☐	☐
Build positive relationships with administrators and support staff	☐ ☐	☐ ☐	☐ ☐
Enjoy social experiences with colleagues outside school	☐	☐	☐
Work with others to build a shared sense of collective efficacy	☐	☐	☐
Seek to moderate high stress levels through individual and group initiatives	☐	☐	☐
As I reflect on my teaching, I			
Set up cooperative learning activities	☐	☐	☐
Encourage class discussions	☐	☐	☐
Emphasize student responsibility	☐	☐	☐
Teach students self-regulation (self-help and self-direction)	☐	☐	☐
Seek out parents and know them by name	☐	☐	☐
Invite parents to participate	☐	☐	☐
Avoid sarcasm and labeling	☐	☐	☐
Convey a clear message that all students can succeed	☐	☐	☐
Persevere with low-achieving students	☐	☐	☐
Hold high but not unreasonable standards for achievement	☐	☐	☐
Choose learning activities that build upon what students already know	☐	☐	☐
Share personal enthusiasm for learning	☐	☐	☐

Qualities Checklist: Caring Indicators

	Yes	Sort of	No
As I reflect on my teaching, either alone or with a colleague, I			
Avoid harsh, punitive measures	☐	☐	☐
Reject behavior, not the student	☐	☐	☐
Nip misbehavior in the bud	☐	☐	☐
Model reflective listening	☐	☐	☐
Look at students when they speak	☐	☐	☐
Expect students to respect me, each other, and themselves	☐	☐	☐
Know students as individuals and know them by name	☐	☐	☐
Emphasize relationships over rules	☐	☐	☐
Talk often with students, inside and outside of class	☐	☐	☐
Am interested in students' lives outside of school	☐	☐	☐
Try to use a variety of teaching strategies	☐	☐	☐
Model for students appropriate ways to deal with frustration	☐	☐	☐
Teach students how to resolve differences	☐	☐	☐
Model respect in the classroom	☐	☐	☐
Model courteous speech	☐	☐	☐
Model concern and empathy	☐	☐	☐

Summary and Conclusion 4

Beyond Great to Memorable

SUMMARY OF SKILLS AND QUALITIES CHECKLISTS

When the checklists in Chapters 2 and 3 (key teacher skills and key teacher qualities checklists) have been completed, responses can be moved to the sections below.

Move a minimum of five strongest skills from the Yes responses in the skills checklist to Section A below and move up a minimum of five strongest qualities from the Yes responses in the efficacy and caring checklists to Section B below.

A. Indicators I listed as Yes from Skills Checklist that are my strongest skill indicators:

_____

_____

_____

_____

_____

B. Indicators I listed as Yes from Qualities Checklist that are my strongest qualities indicators:

_____

_____

_____

_____

_____

These are strong skills and qualities that really do matter and positively affect student achievement and behavior. Copy them into a journal or copy them onto an index card to keep handy while teaching. These quality and skill indicators are your money in the bank. Hold onto them and bravely move into the next area.

Move two Sort of or No skills to Section C below and move two Sort of or No qualities to Section D below.

C. Two items I listed as Sort of or No from my Skills Checklist that I wish to address:

_____

_____

D. Two items I listed as Sort of or No from my Qualities Checklists that I wish to address:

_____

_____

Items listed in Sections C and D will be used below in the Plan of Action.

PLANS OF ACTION

Since I have spoken of social learning theory several times in this book, it is only fitting that I use it once again as a basis for a useful guide to help teachers improve on their skills and qualities. Bandura's social learning theory (1986) relies on *observational learning,* which includes *modeling* (imitating the behavior of others) and *vicarious experience* (observing others succeeding or failing). These measures are integrated into my four-step Basic Plan of Action, which is based on Bandura's model and models of problem solving (identify the problem, make a plan, do it, assess the results). Following the Basic Plan of Action are five Alternate Plans of Action, each of which provides an opportunity to self-assess one's skills and qualities. Last is a follow-up assessment, which is an opportunity to reflect on one's status, progress, and next course of action.

Basic Plan of Action

1. *Identify target skills and qualities.* The teacher identifies which key skills and key qualities she or he wishes to develop. (See Sections C and D directly above.)

2. *Locate a model.* The teacher then locates a colleague or other teacher who can *model* the target skill or quality. This modeling emphasizes vicarious experience; that is, seeing and hearing the model in action and illustrating the target skill or quality. It is important to note that the model has to be simply willing to allow an observer to witness the skill or quality in action. The model does *not* have to be a "model teacher!"

3. *Carry it out.* The teacher then tries out the new behavior. Practice it at least several times, perhaps for a full week.

4. *Assess.* The teacher self-assesses and receives feedback assessment from a colleague or the model. It would be best for the teacher to then model the new behavior for the colleague.

Alternate Plans of Action

Colleague observation and feedback. The optimum learning situation for any teacher includes *another person or persons.* If possible, a trusted colleague can spend time observing in the teacher's classroom. She or he might even take notes during the observation. Afterward, the teacher and colleague meet, preferably at a quiet time such as after school when there is less stress and less pressure to return to the students. The colleague offers specific feedback on what has been observed.

Group discussion and feedback. Another plan of action would involve working cooperatively with a group of peers. Set a time to meet each week with the topic of discussion being the key teacher skills and key teacher qualities. Teachers could do a round robin of observations in which each person in the group observes each other person at least once. This requires a solid sense of trust within the group, so maybe it could be launched by having a dinner together or some other upbeat, nonteaching activity. Another variation would be to work with a partner, where each alternately observes, and then help assess the other. This also calls for a fairly high level of trust, but it may feel safer being with a partner than being part of a group.

Working alone. This is the least desirable strategy, but it can still raise self-awareness. The teacher goes through the process and seeks to observe a model, whether on video or in real life, carrying out the skill or quality. The teacher then seeks to imitate the model and incorporate it into his or her teaching behavior. Journaling may be helpful when working alone.

One-per-month. Another way to address the key skills and qualities would be to go through each of them in order. Take one per month, September through June, and focus exclusively on that one for each month. (This could be done alone, with a partner, or in a group.) For each particular skill or quality area, write the key word on an index card and tape it to an unobtrusive part of your desk or work area. For instance, write the word *Feedback* on the card. During the day, use it as a reminder: "Have I given feedback to students today?" "Has it been specific? Immediate?" You could also ask a respected colleague or model, "How do you give feedback to students in your class? Any ideas you can share with me?"

Videotape and then analyze. Teachers can videotape themselves teaching a lesson, or part of a lesson, and play the tape, analyzing it using the key teacher skills or key teacher qualities. This viewing and analysis can be done in private or with a trusted colleague, mentor, or group. As a supervisor of student teachers, I have found videotaping to be helpful, yet for some student teachers it creates such a high level of arousal (fear and panic) that its usefulness is negated. As a first-year teacher of sixth-grade students, I set up an 8-millimeter movie camera to record my teaching, and it turned out to be a most, um, informative exercise. (Today, that film is long missing.) For the strong-hearted, video can provide a dramatic and rich source of data.

FOLLOW-UP ASSESSMENT

No matter which plan of action is used, later in the term do a simple four-part follow-up assessment for each indicator in your original Sort of or No lists. (Remember to include this on your professional development plan.)

1. Indicator (from original Sort of or No lists):

_____

_____

2. Progress (How I have progressed in this area.)

_____

_____

3. Evidence (What, specifically, do I do different?)

_____

_____

4. Disposition (Should I do more? If so, what?)

_____

_____

CONCLUSION

As I mentioned earlier, there is a lot of concern today about measuring school quality and detecting and penalizing so-called failing schools. Standardized test scores are used to indicate failure, but that is a most inadequate and unfortunate measure. Just as there is a lot more to teaching than numbers, there's a lot more to a school than its standardized test scores. As part of my postdoctoral research project at the University of South Africa, I examined factors that influenced student success, both in academics and in socialization (behavior), and drew up nine guidelines useful in assessing schools and school districts. The guidelines are *qualitative* summary statements of factors that foster student success, and they appear at the end of this book as *Resources*. The guidelines can be useful in assessing how well a school or school district is ensuring student success, or promoting student failure, *without* using standardized test scores. For example, if the school emphasizes academic activity (Guideline 3), that means teachers explicitly convey to students their high expectations for behavior and high expectations for academic work. Research shows that when students are engaged in meaningful activity, behavior problems are rare. (Wouldn't it be so much better if we evaluated our schools based on how well they worked with and for students and for our communities, instead of how high or low their standardized test scores appeared to be compared to some unknowable norm group?)

Improving More Than Yourself

After over 30 years as an educator (and a lifetime as a student), I am convinced that students and teachers are the key players in the education process. Skillful, high-efficacy, and caring teachers are worth the highest acclaim (and salaries!), because they do so much for society. Such teachers teach students knowledge, skills, and attitudes, but their actions also serve to prevent antisocial behavior—and sometimes violent behavior as well—more effectively than medicating students and more effectively than threatening students with harsh consequences. Next in importance only to parents, teachers (and schools themselves) are the best resources any nation has to make inroads into the challenges of ignorance and uncivil behavior. We greatly need skillful, caring teachers and we need to encourage all teachers to strive to become skillful and caring teachers.

The old way doesn't work. We can't keep trying to do it by default; by using our legal system to threaten to remove those unskillful and uncaring teachers. Even if there were no other reason, attempting to remove teachers is frighteningly expensive. In a recent year, New York State attempted to remove 20 allegedly incompetent teachers. The state spent an average of over $175,000 per teacher in legal fees ($317,000 if there was an appeal) in seeking to dismiss those teachers. Zeroing in on 20 teachers and spending over 3 million dollars in an effort to remove them seems like a not-very-cost-effective way to make New York schools (or any schools) better places for students. The threaten-to-fire process simply doesn't help teachers become better teachers, yet it does make lawyers wealthy! The way to build effective teaching lies not in litigation but in education—in teacher preparation before the fact and in providing support and education for teachers before they become teachers (preservice) and while on the job (inservice). We need high-quality teachers rather than the highly qualified teachers mandated by the Leave No Child Behind Act of 2001. The difference is crucial: high quality teachers are skillful and caring and they believe they can and will make a difference in student achievement and behavior. Highly qualified teachers, on the other hand, hold a bachelor's degree, have met requirements for state certification, and know a lot in their content area. True, these three latter requirements are not unimportant, but they fall short—far short—of ensuring the best *quality* teachers for our public schools. Yes, a highly qualified teacher may also be a high-quality teacher and vice versa. But I believe it is more important for a teacher to *know how to teach* (be skilled), *believe that he or she will be successful* because his or her students will be successful (high efficacy), and be a *caring person in the lives of students* than it is for the teacher to simply have the right *qualifications.* Perhaps it will start by our taking back our public schools from the absentee federal and corporate landlords and placing our public schools back in the control of our neighborhoods, communities, towns, and cities.

Taking back our public schools. Due in part to this growing absentee control of public education, our public schools have started to increasingly resemble prisons, and today, with heightened concern about safety, American public schools seem even more prison-like with security guards, police in schools, metal detectors, drug-sniffing dogs, electronic surveillance devices, and all the other trappings of suspicion, mistrust, and fear. Schools as prisons create students as suspects, and such schools are not good places to teach or to learn, nor are they good places to grow people who will make positive contributions to society.

Teaching students content knowledge is important, but, especially today amid heightened fears that the world is not a very safe place, there is a deeper challenge and higher priority facing educators in America and throughout the world: Schools must teach toward a restoration of a sense of human dignity and trust and a restoration of democracy as well. Teachers have been asked to take on huge tasks in the past, and today's tasks have to be the most challenging ever, because solving real problems (like breaking the cycle of war and violence) through education is a formidable task. But even if it takes 100 years, it is a job worth tackling. The old, adversarial methods using fear and punishment have never truly solved a problem, nor have they achieved anything except blind compliance, resentment, and a perpetuation of more fear and punishment. But today we are all living in a new era, a global era where we are more aware of our connections with each other and with the rest of the world. Our public education system, including our schools and teachers, must change to reflect that new awareness and begin to expect *high-quality education* instead of federally mandated *highly qualified education.* The difference is enormous.

South African Archbishop Desmond Tutu (1999, pp. 29–30) speaks of "restorative justice," which seeks not retribution or punishment "but the healing of breaches, the redressing of imbalances, the restoration of broken relationships, and a seeking to rehabilitate both the victims and the perpetrator." That same sense of restoration, and not judgment or revenge, must be the goal of teachers throughout the world—teachers of both the rich and the poor. Many teachers are today showing the leadership for that restoration to occur within our city, suburban, and rural school communities. Toward that end, they must be recognized and further empowered to continue in that direction. The survival of democracy rests on the shoulders of our public schools and its teachers and educators. Author and social critic Neil Postman (1999, p. 334) points directly to the human element in what makes schools successful:

> I do not say, of course, that schools can solve the problems of poverty, alienation and family disintegration, but schools can respond to them. And they can do this because there are people in them, because these people are concerned with more than algebra lessons or modern Japanese history, and because these people can identify not only one's level of competence in math but one's level of rage and confusion and depression.

At the present time, when the American home and family have been weakened and the challenges of fear and violence seem formidable, the hopefulness and restoration provided by great teachers take on special urgency. Thus, it is essential that we get school reform on the right track and not meekly permit vested corporate interests expressed through government initiatives like No Child Left Behind to blot out and minimize what our families, communities, and students really need from our public schools. *They need good teachers, great teachers, and high-quality teachers. They don't need their public schools labeled as "failing," and they don't need those schools closed, but need them improved. Real school improvement starts with great teaching.*

In his autobiography, *My Losing Season,* author Pat Conroy (2002, p. 63) describes how he grew up in a horribly abusive and disfigured household. Conroy describes the solace he found when wonderful teachers were sent into his life and how important these great teachers were in sustaining and encouraging him to find his voice, confidence, and sanity. Conroy said, "The great teachers fill you up with hope and shower you with a thousand reasons to embrace all aspects of life."

Resources

GUIDELINES FOR STUDENT SUCCESS IN ACADEMICS AND SOCIALIZATION: A SCHOOLWIDE QUALITATIVE ASSESSMENT

The following guidelines were drawn from the results of my postdoctoral research project at the University of South Africa titled *A Culture of Violent Behaviour in Contemporary Society: A Socio-Educational Analysis* (DiGiulio, 2001). The guidelines are summary statements of the significant factors that foster student success in both academic achievement and socialization. There are nine guidelines, with explanatory details following each guideline, and boxes are provided so the parts of each guideline might be used as a checklist in a schoolwide or districtwide assessment.

Guideline 1: Promote High-Impact Teaching

☐ Identify and emphasize qualities of high-impact teachers, including caring and teacher efficacy.

☐ Identify and emphasize skills of high-impact teachers, including preparation, attention, clarity, questioning, monitoring, feedback, summarizing, and reflection.

☐ Recognize high-impact teachers and reward those who work with the most difficult of students.

☐ Preservice teachers complete their practice teaching under the instruction of high-impact teachers.

☐ Provide opportunities for all teachers to observe mentor teachers and peer teachers in action.

☐ Reassign teachers who are challenged by antisocial or violent student behavior to work in teams with high-impact teachers.

Guideline 2: Foster Caring Teacher–Student Relationships

☐ Healthy human interpersonal relationships are defined by respect, mutuality, belonging, personal mastery, independence, and dignity.

☐ Emphasize that all human beings have needs to be safe, loved, and accepted and to grow toward self-realization (see Maslow's hierarchy of needs). This is true for teachers as well as students.

☐ Operationally define *caring*, making it part of the job description of teachers, and include it in the evaluations of teachers' performance.

☐ Recognize (identify and acknowledge) teachers who care strongly for students.

☐ Educate future (and present) teachers in ways to show caring *in the students' cultural language* and to be able to show their caring in the *language* and *culture* familiar to the students they will be teaching.

☐ Teachers model appropriate ways of reacting to frustration and anger.

☐ School staff does not use corporal punishment, or other violent measures, against students.

Guideline 3: Emphasize Academic Activity

☐ Teachers explicitly convey to students their high expectations for behavior and high expectations for academic work.

☐ Classroom instruction includes cooperative learning strategies, such as Jigsaw (Slavin, 1990), where each student as part of a group has a different part of the material to be learned and by becoming adept on that part can then teach each other.

☐ Encourage teachers to use social-constructivist instructional learning strategies, which place emphasis on the learner's active engagement in his or her own learning.

☐ Empower students within the safety of the classroom to make choices and have their ideas and products regarded as valued contributions.

Guideline 4: Make Classrooms Communities

☐ Teachers create classrooms that resemble small family-like groups, encouraging classroom discussion and discourse.

☐ All school staff, including classroom teachers, avoid harsh, punitive measures, which are ineffective as deterrents, particularly to students used to a culture of violence.

☐ Educate preservice teachers in ways that create a community in the classroom.

☐ Adopt a classroom ethic of inclusion: All students belong here.

☐ Emphasize cooperation over competition.

☐ Punishment of misbehavior is neither a solution nor a deterrent to future misbehavior.

☐ At every level, the *prevention* of antisocial and violent behavior must take priority over the *punishment* of antisocial or violent behavior.

Guideline 5: Support Teacher Ownership of the Classroom

☐ Communities and administrators support and sustain teacher ownership of classrooms.

☐ Reduce the number of students in each class and in each school.

☐ Administration and local police work together to minimize gang influence in schools and classrooms, where such influence exists and in such difficult circumstances, adopting measures such as class-size reduction and the assignment of two teachers per classroom.

Guideline 6: Seek Clarity With Rules and Expectations

☐ Clearly convey behavioral and academic expectations to students and discuss these fully during the very first days of school.

☐ Set up a classroom system that will ensure that the expectations and rules are practiced and internalized.

☐ Set up classroom procedures that will be congruent with students' cultural communication patterns.

☐ Teachers describe but also model the behavior desired, going beyond mere threats and warnings.

☐ Ensure that rules and expectations do not remain abstract, but become internalized, by having students demonstrate prosocial behaviors.

Guideline 7: Provide Administrative Support by Principal and Support Staff

☐ Schools provide administrative support that is felt personally by the teacher, especially in times of stress and challenge.

☐ Administrators follow through on incidents of violence or serious antisocial behavior.

☐ All schools have a support team available, consisting of the principal or assistant principal, counselor, school psychologist, nurse, and other teachers and, in more violent schools, include police and security guards.

☐ The principal knows each student in school by name and is actively involved with students on a daily basis.

☐ Administration conveys clarity as to each person's role and each person's responsibilities for student behavior.

Guideline 8: Train In-School Police in Violence Prevention and Human Relations

☐ Clearly define the job description and role of police in school to be *supportive* of the education staff, in addition to the traditional police job of apprehending wrongdoers.

☐ If in-school security are present, they must be accessible and responsive to staff and students and particularly responsive to teachers.

☐ Train in-school police in human relations, particularly in child and adolescent development.

Guideline 9: Actively Promote Parent Involvement

☐ Teachers initiate contact with parents, especially parents of students at risk for antisocial and violent behavior.

☐ Teachers spend time talking with all parents and know all parents by their names.

☐ Teachers avoid impersonal methods of communicating with parents, such as through e-mail and written notes, which are less powerful than personal or telephone contact. Besides, parents who most need connection with their child's teacher may simply not have home access to technology more advanced than a telephone.

References

Adams, H. (1999). *The education of Henry Adams.* New York: Bartleby.com. (Original work published 1918) Retrieved July 10, 2003, from http://www.bartleby.com/159/

Allen, J., & Burns, J. (1998). Research report: Managing inclusive classrooms. *Kappa Delta Phi Record, 35,* 28–30.

Allinder, R. M. (1994). The relationship between efficacy and the instructional practices of special education teachers and consultants. *Teacher Education and Special Education, 17,* 86–95.

Allington, R. L., & Johnston, P. H. (2000). What do we know about effective fourth-grade teachers and their classrooms? CELA (Center on English Learning and Achievement) Report. Albany: National Research Center on English Learning and Achievement, University at Albany, State University of New York. (ERIC Report No. ED447404)

American Psychological Association. (1993). *Violence and youth: Psychology's response.* American Psychological Association Commission on Violence and Youth (Vol. 1). Washington, DC: Author.

Anderson, L., & Krathwohl, D. (Eds.). (2001). *A taxonomy for learning, teaching, and assessing: A revision of Bloom's Taxonomy of Educational Objectives.* New York: Addison Wesley Longman.

Anderson, V., & Hidi, S. (1988/1989). Teaching students to summarize. *Educational Leadership, 46*(4), 26–28.

Archer, A. (1990–1994). Skills for school success. North Billerica, MA: Curriculum Associates.

Armstrong, T. (2000). *Multiple intelligences in the classroom* (2nd ed.). Alexandria, VA: Association for Supervision and Curriculum Development.

Ascher, C., & Fruchter, N. (2001). Teacher quality and student performance in New York City's low-performing schools. *Journal of Education for Students Placed at Risk, 6*(3), 199–215.

Ashton, P. T., & Webb, R. B. (1986). *Making a difference: Teachers' sense of efficacy and student achievement.* New York: Longman.

Astor, R., Meyer, H., & Behre, W. (1999). Unowned places and times: Maps and interviews about violence in high schools. *American Educational Research Journal, 8,* 3–42.

Azrin, N. H., Hake, D. G., Holz, W. C., & Hutchinson, R. R. (1965). Motivational aspects of escape from punishment. *Journal of the Experimental Analysis of Behavior, 8,* 31–34.

Bandura, A. (1977). *Social learning theory.* Englewood Cliffs, NJ: Prentice Hall.

Bandura, A. (1986). *Social foundations of thought and action: A social cognitive theory.* Upper Saddle River, NJ: Prentice Hall.

Bandura, A. (1993). Perceived self-efficacy in cognitive development and functioning. *Educational Psychologist, 28,* 117–148.

Bandura, A. (1997). *Self-efficacy: The exercise of control.* New York: Freeman.

Baumrind, D. (1989). Rearing competent children. In W. Damon (Ed.), *New directions for child development: Adolescent health and human development* (pp. 349–378). San Francisco: Jossey-Bass.

Beck, F. W. (1981). Training in attention: A case study. *Journal for Special Educators, 17,* 366–370.

Becker, R. R. (2000). The critical role of students' questions in literacy development. *Educational Forum, 64,* 261–271.

Beginning Teacher Support and Assessment, California Department of Education. Retrieved September 11, 2003, from http://www.btsa.ca.gov/

Berkowitz, L. (1983). Aversively stimulated aggression: Some parallels and difference in research with animals and humans. *American Psychologist, 38,* 1135–1144.

Black, S. (2001). Ask me a question: How teachers use inquiry in a classroom. *American School Board Journal, 188*(5), 43–45.

Blake, D. A. (1996). "Chat-backs" engage students. *Education Digest, 61*(9), 54–55.

Bloom, B. S., Englehart, M. D., Furst, E. J., Hill, W. H., & Krathwohl, D. R. (1956). *Taxonomy of educational objectives. The classification of educational goals: Handbook I, Cognitive domain.* New York: David McKay.

Bracey, G. W. (2003). April foolishness: The 20th anniversary of *A Nation at Risk. Phi Delta Kappan, 84,* 616–621.

Brigham, F. J., Scruggs, T. E., & Mastropieri, M. A. (1992). Teacher enthusiasm in learning disabilities classrooms: effects on learning and behavior. *Learning Disabilities Research and Practice, 7,* 68–73.

Brighton, K. (1998). The standards frenzy: The latest challenge to authentic learning at the middle level. *Journal of the New England League of Middle Schools, 11,* 1–3.

Brophy, J. (1996). Enhancing students' socialization: Key elements. *ERIC Digest.* (ERIC No. ED395713) Retrieved September 13, 2003 from http://askeric. org/Eric/

Brophy, J., & Good, T. L. (1986). Teacher behavior and student achievement. In M. C. Wittrock (Ed.), *Handbook of research on teaching: A project of the American Educational Research Association* (pp. 328–375). New York: Simon & Schuster Macmillan.

Butler, D. L., & Winne, P. H. (1995). Feedback and self-regulated learning: A theoretical synthesis. *Review of Educational Research, 65,* 245–281.

Campbell, J. R. (1974). Can a teacher really make the difference? *School Science and Mathematics, 74,* 657–666.

Cantor, J., Kester, D., & Miller, A. (2000). *Amazing results! Teacher expectations and student achievement (TESA) follow-up survey of TESA-trained teachers in 45 states and the District of Columbia.* Paper presented at the annual meeting of the California Educational Research Association, Santa Barbara, CA.

Carlisle, C., & Phillips, D. A. (1984). The effects of enthusiasm training on selected teacher and student behaviors in preservice physical education teachers. *Journal of Teaching in Physical Education, 4,* 64–75.

Carlson, M. O., Humphrey, G. E., & Reinhardt, K. S. (2003) *Weaving science inquiry and continuous assessment.* Thousand Oaks, CA: Corwin Press.

Cartledge G., & Milburn, J. (1978). The case for teaching social skills in the classroom: A review. *Review of Educational Research, 48,* 133–156.

Caruso, V. M. (1982). Enthusiastic teaching. *Journal of Physical Education, Recreation and Dance, 53,* 47–48.

Cazden, C. B. (1986). Classroom discourse. In M. C. Wittrock (Ed.), *Handbook of research on teaching: A project of the American Educational Research Association* (pp. 432–463). New York: Simon & Schuster Macmillan.

Chester, M. D., & Beaudin, B. Q. (1996). Efficacy beliefs of newly hired teachers in urban schools. *American Educational Research Journal, 44,* 233–257.

Chin, C., Brown, D. E., & Bruce, B. C. (2002). Student-generated questions: A meaningful aspect of learning in science. *International Journal of Science Education, 24,* 521–549.

Clark, C. M., & Peterson, P. L. (1986). Teachers' thought processes. In M. C. Wittrock (Ed.), *Handbook of research on teaching: A project of the American Educational Research Association* (pp. 255–296). New York: Simon & Schuster Macmillan.

Cole, A. (2003, March 12). It's the teacher, not the program. *Education Week.* Retrieved April 5, 2003 from http://www.edweek.org/ew/ewstory.cfm?slug=26cole.h22

Collinson, V., Killeavy, M., & Stephenson, H. J. (1998, April 13–17). *Exemplary teachers: Practicing an ethic of care in England, Ireland, and the United States.* Paper presented at the annual meeting of the American Educational Research Association, San Diego, CA.

Conroy, P. (2002). *My losing season.* New York: Bantam.

Cotton, K. (1988, May). School Improvement Research Series Close-up #4: Monitoring student learning in the classroom. Retrieved September 10, 2003, from http://www.nwrel.org/scpd/sirs/2/cu4.html

Council of Chief State School Officers. (2003, July 11). *Andy Baumgartner 1999 National Teacher of the Year.* Retrieved September 16, 2003, from http://www.ccsso.org/Projects/national_teacher_of_the_year/national_teachers/187.cfm

Cummings, C. (1990). *Teaching makes a difference* (2nd ed.). Edmonds, WA: Teaching, Inc.

Danielson, C. (1996). *Enhancing professional practice: A framework for teaching.* Alexandria, VA: Association for Supervision and Curriculum Development.

Darling-Hammond, L. (1995). Changing conceptions of teaching and teacher development. *Teacher Education Quarterly, 22*(4), 9–26.

Darling-Hammond, L. (2003). How teacher education matters. In J. W. Noll (Ed.), *Taking sides: Clashing views on controversial educational issues* (12th ed., pp. 390–399). Guilford, CT: McGraw-Hill/Dushkin.

Darling-Hammond, L., & Youngs, P. (2002). Defining "highly-qualified teachers": What does "scientifically-based research" actually tell us? *Educational Researcher, 31*(9), 13–25.

Dempster, F. (1991). Synthesis of research on reviews and tests. *Educational Leadership, 48*(7), 71–76.

DiGiulio, R. (2000). *Positive classroom management* (2nd ed.). Thousand Oaks, CA: Corwin Press.

DiGiulio, R. (2001). *A culture of violent behavior in contemporary society: A socio-educational analysis.* Unpublished doctoral thesis, University of South Africa, Pretoria. Available from the University of South Africa Library through http://oasis.unisa.ac.za/

Donald, J. (2000, April 24–28). *Indicators of success: From concepts to classrooms.* Paper presented at the annual meeting of the American Educational Research Association, New Orleans, LA.

Doyle, W. (1977). Learning in the classroom environment: An ecological analysis. *Journal of Teacher Education, 28,* 51–55.

Doyle, W. (1983). Academic work. *Review of Educational Research, 53,* 159–200.

Doyle, W. (1986). Classroom organization and management. In M. C. Wittrock (Ed.), *Handbook of research on teaching: A project of the American Educational Research Association* (pp. 392–432). New York: Simon & Schuster Macmillan.

Dyck, B. A. (2002, August). Using technology to support professional reflection. Retrieved September 11, 2003 from http://www.sasinschool.com/resource/pages/ethread_reflection.shtml

Eder, D. (1982). Differences in communicative styles across ability groups. In L. C. Wilkinson (Ed.), *Communicating in classrooms* (pp. 245–264). New York: Academic Press.

Edwards, S., & Bowman, M. A. (1996). Promoting student learning through questioning: A study of classroom questions. *Journal on Excellence in College Teaching, 7*(2), 3–24.

Eggen, P., & Kauchak, D. (2001). *Educational psychology: Windows on classrooms* (5th ed.). Upper Saddle River, NJ: Merrill Prentice Hall.

Eggen, P., & Kauchak, D. (2004). *Educational psychology: Windows on classrooms* (6th ed.). Upper Saddle River, NJ: Merrill Prentice Hall.

Elliott, D. S., Hamburg, B. A., & Williams, K. R. (1998). *Violence in American schools.* Cambridge, UK: Cambridge University Press.

Ellis, K. (1993). *Teacher questioning behavior and student learning: What research says to teachers.* Paper presented at the 1993 Convention of the Western States Communication Association, Albuquerque, NM.

Emmer, E. T., & Gerwels, M. C. (2002). Cooperative learning in elementary classrooms: Teaching practices and lesson characteristics. *Elementary School Journal, 103,* 75–91.

Epstein, J. L. (1990). School and family connections: Theory, research, and implications for integrating sociologies of education and family. *Marriage & Family Review, 48,* 99–126.

Evertson, C. M., Emmer, E. T., & Brophy, J. E. (1980, May). Predictors of effective teaching in junior high mathematics classrooms. *Journal for Research in Mathematics, 11,* 161–178.

Fast, J. (1970). *Body language.* New York: MJF Books.

Fisher, C., Berliner, D., Filby, N., Marliave, R., Cohen, K., & Dishaw, M. (1980). Teaching behaviors, academic learning time, and student achievement: An overview. In *Time to learn* (pp. 7–32). Washington, DC: National Institute of Education.

Gall, M. D. (1970). The use of questions in teaching. *Review of Educational Research, 40,* 707–721.

Galper, J. (1998). Schooling for society: A swiftly changing scene. *American Demographics, 20*(3), 33.

Gardner, H. (1993). *Multiple intelligences: The theory in practice.* New York: Basic Books.

Garet, M. S., Porter, A. C., Desimone, L., Birman, B. F., & Suk Yoon, K. (2001). What makes professional development effective? Results from a national sample of teachers. *American Educational Research Journal, 38,* 915–945.

Gettinger, M. (1995). Best practices for increasing academic learning time. In A. Thomas & J. Grimes (Eds.), *Best practice in school psychology* (Vol. 3, pp. 943–954). Washington, DC: National Association of School Psychologists.

Gettinger, M., & Stoiber, K. C. (1999). Excellence in teaching: Review of instructional and environmental variables. In C. R. Reynolds & T. B. Gutkin (Eds.), *The handbook of school psychology* (3rd ed., pp. 933–958). New York: John Wiley.

Gibson, S., & Dembo, M. (1984). Teacher efficacy: A construct validation. *Journal of Educational Psychology, 76,* 569–582.

Gijselaers, W. H., & Schmidt, H. G. (1995). Effects of quantity of instruction on time spent on learning and achievement. *Educational Research and Evaluation, 1,* 183–201.

Ginott, H. G. (1972). *Teacher and child.* New York: Avon.

Goddard, R. D., & Goddard, Y. L. (2001, April). *An exploration of the relationship between collective efficacy and teacher efficacy.* Paper presented at the annual meeting of the American Educational Research Association, Seattle, WA.

Goddard, R. D., Hoy, W. K., & Woolfolk Hoy, A. (2000). Collective teacher efficacy: Its meaning, measure, and impact on student achievement. *American Educational Research Journal, 37,* 479–507.

Good, T., & Brophy, J. (2000). *Looking in classrooms* (8th ed.). New York: Longman.

Graham, S., MacArthur, C., & Schwartz, S. (1995). Effects of goal setting and procedural facilitation on the revising behavior and writing performance of students with writing and learning problems. *Journal of Educational Psychology, 87*(2), 230–240.

Green, L., Fry, A. F., & Myerson, J. (1994). Discounting of delayed rewards: A life-span comparison. *Psychological Science, 5,* 33–36.

Grill, J. J. (1981). Are we asking the right questions? *Academic Therapy, 16,* 365–369.

Hamaker, C. (1986). The effects of adjunct questions on prose learning. *Review of Educational Research, 56,* 212–242.

Hamilton, R. J. (1985). A framework for the evaluation of the effectiveness of adjunct questions and objectives. *Review of Educational Research, 55,* 47–85.

Harmin, M. (1994). *Inspiring active learning: A handbook for teachers.* Alexandria, VA: Association for Supervision and Curriculum Development.

Harper, C. B. J. (1976, May 10–14). *The importance of attending behavior in learning to read.* Paper presented at the 21st annual meeting of the International Reading Association, Anaheim, CA.

Haycock, K. (1998a, August 10). Good teaching matters . . . a lot. *Education Trust.* Retrieved September 9, 2003, from http://www2.edtrust.org/EdTrust/Press+Room/good+teaching.htm

Haycock, K. (1998b, Summer). Good teaching matters: How well-qualified teachers can close the gap. *Thinking K-16, 3*(2). (ERIC Report No. ED457260) Washington, DC: Education Trust.

Hines, C. V., Cruickshank, D. R., & Kennedy, J. J. (1982, March). *Measures of teacher clarity and their relationships to student achievement and satisfaction.* Paper presented at the annual meeting of the American Educational Research Association, New York.

Holland, R. (2003). How to build a better teacher. In J. W. Noll (Ed.), *Taking sides: Clashing views on controversial educational issues* (12th ed., pp. 380–389). Guilford, CT: McGraw-Hill/Dushkin.

Houston, P. (2000, November). A conversation with Kozol. *School Administrator.* Retrieved September 1, 2003 from http://www.aasa.org/publications/sa/2000_11/Kozol.htm

Huff, C. R. (1989). Youth gangs and public policy. *Crime & Delinquency, 35,* 524–537.

Hunter, M. (1990–1991). Lesson design helps achieve the goals of science instruction. *Educational Leadership, 48*(4), 79–81.

Johnson State College Education Department. (2003–2004). *Student teaching handbook: Engaged in creative teaching and learning.* Johnson, VT: Author.

Kagan, D. (1992). Implications of research on teacher beliefs. *Educational Psychologist, 27,* 65–90.

Kearsley, I. (2002). Build on the rock: Teacher feedback and reader competence. *Australian Journal of Language and Literacy, 25,* 8–25.

Kerman, S. (1979). Teacher expectations and students achievement. *Phi Delta Kappan, 60,* 70–72.

Kindsvatter, R., Wilen, W., & Ishler, M. (1988). *Dynamics of effective teaching.* New York: Longman.

King, A. (1992). Comparison of self-questioning, summarizing, and notetaking—review as strategies for learning from lectures. *American Educational Research Journal, 29,* 303–323.

Kleinfeld, J. (1983). *Doing research on effective cross-cultural teaching: The teacher tale.* Fairbanks, AK: Alaska University, Fairbanks Institute of Social, Economic, and Government Research.

Kohn, A. (1993). *Punished by rewards.* Boston: Houghton Mifflin.

Kounin, J. (1970). *Discipline and group management in classrooms.* New York: Holt, Rinehart & Winston.

Kramer-Schlosser, L. (1992). Teacher distance and student disengagement: School lives on the margin. *Journal of Teacher Education, 43*(20), 128–140.

Krathwohl, D. R., Bloom, B. S., & Masia, B. B. (1964) *Taxonomy of educational objectives: Handbook II: Affective domain.* New York: David McKay.

Kulik, J. A., & Kulik, C. C. (1988). Timing of feedback and verbal learning. *Review of Educational Research, 58,* 79–97.

Land, M. L. (1979). Low-inference variables of teacher clarity: Effects on student concept learning. *Journal of Educational Psychology, 71,* 795–799.

Language and Learning Improvement Branch, Division of Instruction. (n.d.). Maryland State Department of Education, Office of Library Information Services, Baltimore County Public Schools. Retrieved September 10, 2003 from http://www.bcps.org/offices/lis/office/inst/questthinking.html

Leven, T., & Long, R. (1981). *Effective instruction.* Washington, DC: Association for Supervision and Curriculum Development.

Lewis, R., Berghoff, R., & Pheeney, P. (1999). Focusing students: Three approaches for learning through evaluation. *Innovative Higher Education, 23*(3), 181–196.

Lhyle, K. G., & Kulhavy, R.W. (1987). Feedback processing and error correction. *Journal of Educational Psychology, 79,* 320–322.

Linik, J. (2002). Nothing but the best: At Grant Elementary, teachers expect their multiethnic students to strive for the top. *Northwest Education, 8,* 40–45.

Little, J. W. (1993). Teachers' professional development in a climate of educational reform. *Educational Evaluation and Policy Analysis, 15,* 129–151.

Loucks-Horsley, S., Hewson, P. W., Love, N., & Stiles, K. E. (1998). *Designing professional development for teachers of science and mathematics.* Thousand Oaks, CA: Corwin Press.

Luster, T., & McAdoo, H. P. (1994). Factors related to the achievement and adjustment of young African-American children. *Child Development, 65,* 1080–1094.

Marjoribanks, K., & Mboya, M. M. (1998). Factors affecting the self-concepts of South African students. *Journal of Social Psychology, 138,* 572–580.

Marks, H. M. (2000). Student engagement in instructional activity: Patterns in the elementary, middle, and high school years. *American Educational Research Journal, 37,* 153–184.

Marlowe, B. A., & Page, M. L. (1998). *Creating and sustaining the constructivist classroom.* Thousand Oaks, CA: Corwin Press.

Martin, J. R. (1992). *The schoolhome.* Cambridge, MA: Harvard University Press.

Matsumura, L. C., Patthey-Chavez, G. G., Valeds, R., & Garnier, H. (2002). Teacher feedback, writing assignment quality, and third-grade students' revision in lower- and higher-achieving urban schools. *Elementary School Journal, 103,* 3–26.

Mayer, G. R. (1995). Preventing antisocial behavior in the schools. *Journal of Applied Behavior Analysis, 28,* 467–478.

McCloskey, R. (1941). *Make way for ducklings.* New York: Viking.

McCombs, B. L., & Marzano, R. J. (1990). Putting the self in self-regulated learning: The self as agent in integrating skill and will. *Educational Psychologist, 25,* 51–70.

McFadden, A. C., Marsh, G. E., Price, B. J., & Hwang, Y. (1992). A study of race and gender bias in the punishment of school children. *Education and Treatment of Children, 15,* 140–146.

McKenzie, J. (2000). *Beyond technology: Questioning, research and the information literate school.* Bellingham, WA: FNO Press.

Meijer, C., & Foster, S. (1988). The effect of teacher self-efficacy on referral chance. *Journal of Special Education, 22,* 378–385.

Montessori, M. (1964). *The Montessori method.* New York: Schocken.

Montessori, M. (1966). *The secret of childhood.* New York: Ballantine.

Moore, W. L., & Cooper, H. (1984). Correlations between teacher and student backgrounds and teacher perceptions of discipline problems and disciplinary techniques. *Discipline, 5,* 1–7.

Morine-Dershimer, G. (1987). Can we talk? In D. Berliner & B. Rosenshine (Eds.), *Talks to teachers* (pp. 37–53). New York: Random House.

Munk, D. D., & Repp, A. C. (1994). The relationship between instructional variables and problem behavior: A review. *Exceptional Children, 60,* 390–401.

Myles, B. S., & Simpson, R. L. (1998). Aggression and violence by school-age children and youth: Understanding the aggression cycle and prevention/intervention strategies. *Intervention in School and Clinic, 33,* 259–264.

O'Donnell, J., Hawkins, J. D., & Abbott, R. D. (1995). Predicting serious delinquency and substance use among aggressive boys. *Journal of Consulting and Clinical Psychology, 63,* 529–537.

Olina, Z., & Sullivan, H. (2002, April). *Effects of teacher and self-assessment on student performance.* Paper presented at the annual meeting of the American Educational Research Association, New Orleans, LA.

Ormrod, J. E. (2004). *Human learning.* Upper Saddle River, NJ: Pearson Education.

Ovando, C. J. (2001). Beyond "blaming the victim": Successful schools for Latino students. *Educational Researcher, 30*(3), 29–31, 39.

Pellett, T. L., Henschel-Pellett, H. A., & Harrison, J. M. (1994). Feedback effects: Field-based findings. *Journal of Physical Education, Recreation & Dance, 65*(9), 75–78.

Perez, S. (2000). An ethic of caring in teaching culturally diverse students. *Education, 121,* 102–105.

Perry, R. (1985). Instructor expressiveness: Implications for improving teaching. In J. Donald & A. Sullivan (Eds.), *Using research to improve teaching* (pp. 35–49). San Francisco: Jossey-Bass.

Peterson, P. L., & Clark, C. M. (1978). Teachers' report of their cognitive processes during teaching. *American Educational Research Journal, 15,* 555–565.

Piper, W. (pseud.) (1930). *The little engine that could.* New York: Platt & Munk.

Postman, N. (1999). Virtual students, digital classrooms. In J. W. Noll (Ed.), *Taking sides: Clashing views on controversial education issues* (pp. 329–335). Guilford, CT: Dushkin/McGraw Hill.

Purkey, S., & Smith, M. (1983). Effective schools: A review. *Elementary School Journal, 83,* 427–452.

Putnam, D. (1895). *A manual of pedagogics.* New York: Silver, Burdett.

Richardson, V. (1990). Significant and worthwhile change in teaching practice. *Educational Research, 19,* 10–18.

Rinehart, S. D., Stahl, S. A., & Erickson, L. G. (1986). Some effects of summarization training on reading and studying. *Reading Research Quarterly, 21,* 422–438.

Rose, L. C., & Gallup, A. M. (2003, September). The 35th Annual Phi Delta Kappa/Gallup Poll of the public's attitudes toward the public schools. *Phi Delta Kappan, 85,* 41–56.

Rosenshine, B., & Furst, N. (1973). The use of direct observation to study teaching. In R. M. W. Travers (Ed.), *Second handbook of research on teaching* (pp. 122–183). Chicago: Rand McNally.

Rosenshine, B., Meister, C., & Chapman, S. (1996). Teaching students to generate questions: A review of the intervention studies. *Review of Educational Research, 66,* 181–221.

Rosenshine, B., & Stevens, R. (1986). Teaching functions. In M. C. Wittrock (Ed.), *Handbook of research on teaching: A project of the American Educational Research Association* (pp. 376–391). New York: Simon & Schuster Macmillan.

Ross, E. W., & Mathison, S. (2002, January 2). No child left untested. *Courier-Journal (Louisville, KY),* p. A7.

Rowe, M. (1986). Wait-time: Slowing down may be a way of speeding up. *Journal of Teacher Education, 37,* 43–50.

Royal Bank of Canada. (1989, September/October). The importance of teaching. *Royal Bank Letter, 70*(5), 1–4.

Rutter, M., Maughan, B., Morimore, R., Outson, J., & Smith, A. (1982). *Fifteen thousand hours.* Cambridge, MA: Harvard University Press.

Sanders, B. (1994). *A is for ox: Violence, electronic media, and the silencing of the written word.* New York: Pantheon.

Sanders, W. (2003). *Teachers, teachers, teachers!* Retrieved April 26, 2003 from http://www.ndol.org/blueprint/fall/99/solutions4.html

Schmuck, P., & Schmuck, R. (1992). *Group processes in the classroom* (6th ed.). Dubuque, IA: Brown.

Sergiovanni, T. (1994). *Building community in schools.* San Francisco: Jossey-Bass.

Shapiro, S. (1993). Strategies that create a positive classroom environment. *Clearing House, 67*(7), 91.

Shaw, S. R., & Braden, J. P. (1990). Race and gender bias in the administration of corporal punishment. *School Psychology Review, 19,* 378–383.

Shechtman, Z. (1997). Enhancing social relationships and adjusting behavior in the Israeli classroom. *Journal of Educational Research, 91*(2), 99–107.

Shuell, T. (1996). Teaching and learning in a classroom context. In D. Berliner & R. Calfee (Eds.), *Handbook of educational psychology* (pp. 726–764). New York: Macmillan.

Shultz, J., & Florio, S. (1979). Stop and freeze: The negotiation of social and physical space in a kindergarten/first grade classroom. *Anthropology and Education Quarterly, 10*(3), 166–181.

Slavin, R. (1990). *Co-operative learning.* Englewood Cliffs, NJ: Prentice Hall.

Slavin, R. (1994). *A practical guide to cooperative learning.* Boston: Allyn & Bacon.

Slavin, R. (2003). *Educational psychology: Theory and practice* (7th ed.). Boston: Allyn & Bacon.

Slavin, R. (n.d.). *A model of effective instruction.* Center for Research on the Education of Students Placed at Risk, Johns Hopkins University. Retrieved September 4, 2003, from http://www.successforall.net/resource/research/modeleffect.htm

Stipek, D. J. (1993). *Motivation to learn: From theory to practice* (2nd ed.). Needham Heights, MA: Allyn & Bacon.

Stipek, D. J. (1996). Motivation and instruction. In D. C. Berliner & R. C. Calfee (Eds.), *Handbook of educational psychology.* New York: Macmillan.

Thayer-Bacon, B. J. (1999). How can caring help? A personalized cross-generational examination of violent adolescent experiences in school. In L. R. Forcey & I. M. Harris (Eds.), *Peacebuilding for adolescents: Strategies for educators and community leaders* (pp. 139–160). New York: Peter Lang.

Thiede, K. W., & Anderson, M. C. M. (2003). Summarizing can improve meta-cognitive accuracy. *Contemporary Educational Psychology, 28,* 129–160.

Thomas, M. D., & Bainbridge, W. L. (2002). No Child Left Behind: Facts and fallacies. *Phi Delta Kappan, 83,* 781–782.

Tobin, K., & Capie, W. (1980). The effects of teacher wait time and questioning quality on middle school science achievement. *Journal of Research in Science Teaching, 17,* 469–475.

Traina, R. P. (1999). What makes a good teacher? *Education Week on the Web, 18*(19), 34. Retrieved March 18, 2003, from http://www.edweek.org/ew/ewstory.cfm?slug=19traina.h18&keywords=Traina

Tutu, D. (1999). No future without forgiveness. *New Perspectives Quarterly, 16*(5), 29–30.

U.S. Department of Education. (2003). *No Child Left Behind: A toolkit for teachers.* Retrieved September 18, 2003, from http://www.ed.gov/teachers/nclbguide/index2.html

Walberg, H. (1988). Synthesis of research on time and learning. *Educational Leadership, 46*(6), 76–80.

Wang, M., Haertel, G., & Walberg, H. (1993). Toward a knowledge base for school learning. *Review of Educational Research, 63*(3), 249–294.

Waterfield, R. A. H. (1987). Plato, *Theaetetus.* (R. A. H. Waterfield, Trans.). London: Penguin.

Waxman, H. C., & Walberg, H. J. (Eds.). (1991). *Effective teaching: Current research.* Berkeley, CA: McCutchan.

Wigfield, A. (1988). Children's attributions for success and failure: Effects of age and attentional focus. *Journal of Educational Psychology, 80*, 76–81.

Wilson, S. M., & Berne, J. (1999). Teacher learning and the acquisition of professional knowledge: An examination of research on contemporary professional development. In A. Iran-Nejad & P. D. Pearson (Eds.), *Review of research in education,* Vol. 24 (pp. 173–209). Washington, DC: American Educational Research Association.

Wood, D., Bruner, J., & Ross, S. (1976). The role of tutoring in problem solving. *British Journal of Psychology, 66*, 181–196.

Woolfolk, A., & Hoy, W. K. (1990). Prospective teachers' sense of efficacy and beliefs about control. *Journal of Educational Psychology, 82*, 81–91.

Woolfolk, A. E. (1993). *Educational psychology* (5th ed.). Needham Heights, MA: Allyn & Bacon.

Woolfolk, A. E. (2001). *Educational psychology* (8th ed.). New York: Allyn & Bacon.

Index

**CORWIN
PRESS**

The Corwin Press logo—a raven striding across an open book—represents the union of courage and learning. Corwin Press is committed to improving education for all learners by publishing books and other professional development resources for those serving the field of K-12 education. By providing practical, hands-on materials, Corwin Press continues to carry out the promise of its motto: **"Helping Educators Do Their Work Better."**